# Praise for *Miracles Amongst Us*

*Miracles Amongst Us* offers a great insight into the life of Jesus when He was on earth. The book portrays the miracles He performed then and the miracles He performs today through the Holy Spirit and the protection of His angels. It's apparent they are working through Mike as he ministers to his family, church, and prison ministry. I pray that anyone who reads this book will want to walk with the Lord Jesus on earth and in Heaven.

– Jim Roberts, former Fire Captain - OKC; Founder, Fellowship of Christian Firefighters - OKC; follower of Christ 64 years

In his book, *Miracles Amongst Us*, Mike Mayo challenges us to consider the events in our lives that can be explained by nothing less than God's intervention. He passionately explores not only Old Testament prophecies of a coming Messiah, but also some of the miracles performed by that incarnate Messiah, which sets the stage for examples of miraculous events that have occurred in Mike's life and to a few of his friends. Mike's passion for sharing what God has done in his life is evident on every page of this book, as each story is sure to cause the reader to realize that miracles do happen, often when we least expect them.

– Steve Golding, former President of Jackson-Shaw Company and Dallas Seminary Foundation

Mike wants us to know Jesus and trust Him. This book is evidence of that truth. Mike's book strengthens our faith by putting us on the map with thoughtful scripture, miracles, and real stories about trust, hope, and perseverance.

– Jeff Waychoff, former Regional Vice President (retired) of Stanley Black & Decker, and a Shepherd Leader at BSF

*Miracles Amongst Us* is more than an inspiring remembrance of the miraculous acts of God as attested to in the biblical accounts of the Old Testament and the miracles of Jesus in the New Testament. It continues with moving miraculous acts of God in today's world. This is a book of inspiration, hope, and wonder that reminds us who God is and how he loves us.

– John Robinson, former Senior Vice President & General Manager of a division of Nokia; currently involved with starting a new church plant: Lake Kiowa Fellowship, Lake Kiowa, TX

This is a book that every believer should read, regardless of where they are on their faith journey. It is about the hope we have in Jesus Christ and the confirmation that God is sovereign and has a specific plan for us all. Mike does a terrific job of starting with scripture, then transitioning to personal experiences with him and his friends that validate this sovereign plan.

– R. Scott Dennis, CEO of Invesco Private Markets

Anyone interested in having a more experiential relationship with the work and power of the Holy Spirit will find this book a helpful and thought-provoking read. Mike organizes the miraculous works of God into a practical, easy-to-understand way that opens the reader's mind and heart to a God who loves them enough to be present in tangible ways.

– Darin Sloan, Coach, Teacher, and Entrepreneur

# MIRACLES AMONGST US

# MIRACLES
## AMONGST US

BEFORE, THEN, *and* NOW

**MIKE E. MAYO**

Miracles Amongst Us

Copyright © 2025 by Mike Mayo

All rights reserved. No part of this book may be reproduced or used in any manner without written permission of the copyright owner, except for the use of quotations in a book review.

ISBN (hardcover): 978-1-968737-04-7

ISBN (paperback): 978-1-968737-00-9

ISBN (ebook): 978-1-968737-01-6

Library of Congress Control Number: 2025949210

Scriptures are taken from the NEW INTERNATIONAL VERSION (NIV): Scripture taken from THE HOLY BIBLE, NEW INTERNATIONAL VERSION®. Copyright© 1973, 1978, 1984, 2011 by Biblica, Inc.™. Used by permission of Zondervan.
Scriptures marked KJV are taken from the KING JAMES VERSION (KJV): KING JAMES VERSION, public domain.

Cover images by: Mike Mayo, Anastasiya D
Original maps by: LeandroPP/istock (Jerusalem City, Map of the Divided Kingdom, New Babylonian Empire and Egyptian Kingdom), Hey Darlin/istock (Texas, Colorado), PeterHermesFurian/istock (Australasia, Australia and New Zealand, subregion of Oceania)
Cover and interior design, map customization, and typesetting by youngdesign.biz

BookJourney

Published by Book Journey Publishing | Bookjourney.com
Castle Rock, Colorado, USA

*Dedicated to my six grandchildren:*

*Everleigh Ann Mayo*
*Harper Elizabeth Mayo*
*Holland Michelle Mayo*
*Reese Jeanne Mayo*
*John Michael William Mayo*
*Wren Marcia Mayo*

# Contents

*Preface, ix*

**Section One** Messianic Prophecies Fulfilled in the New Testament
1. Born in Bethlehem . . . . . . . . . . . . . . . . . . . . . 3
2. Born of a Virgin . . . . . . . . . . . . . . . . . . . . . . 7
3. Riding on a Donkey . . . . . . . . . . . . . . . . . . . 11
4. Betrayed for Thirty Pieces of Silver . . . . . . . . . 15
5. An Offering for Our Sins . . . . . . . . . . . . . . . . 19
6. Death by Crucifixion . . . . . . . . . . . . . . . . . . . 23
7. Jesus Foretold of His Death and Resurrection 29
8. The Timing of His Death . . . . . . . . . . . . . . . 39

**Section Two** Miracles by Jesus
9. Water into Wine . . . . . . . . . . . . . . . . . . . . . . 47
10. He Heals a Son . . . . . . . . . . . . . . . . . . . . . . . 51
11. He Heals a Lame Man . . . . . . . . . . . . . . . . . 55
12. He Feeds Five Thousand . . . . . . . . . . . . . . . 61
13. He Walks on Water . . . . . . . . . . . . . . . . . . . 67
14. He Heals a Blind Man . . . . . . . . . . . . . . . . . 71
15. He Raises Lazarus . . . . . . . . . . . . . . . . . . . . 79
16. Resurrection . . . . . . . . . . . . . . . . . . . . . . . . 87

**Section Three** Modern-Day Miracles

17. God's Provisions . . . . . . . . . . . . . . . . . . . . . . . 95
18. The Long Awakening. . . . . . . . . . . . . . . . . . . .103
19. Modern-Day Lazarus. . . . . . . . . . . . . . . . . . . .119
20. Do You Believe in Angels? . . . . . . . . . . . . . . .129
21. Our Protector . . . . . . . . . . . . . . . . . . . . . . . . .133
22. Conviction . . . . . . . . . . . . . . . . . . . . . . . . . . .137
23. Ronald McDonald House . . . . . . . . . . . . . . .141
24. Behind the Wire . . . . . . . . . . . . . . . . . . . . . . 147

*Closing Words, 151*
*Acknowledgments, 155*
*References, 159*
*About the Author, 161*

# *Preface*

HAVE YOU EVER WONDERED HOW animals, insects, fish, and birds migrate thousands of miles annually and then know how to return to the exact same spot year after year? Ducks, geese, salmon, sea turtles, wildebeest, whales, homing pigeons, honeybees, salamanders, lobsters, caribou, monarch butterflies, dolphins, and many more species have an ability called magnetoreception. This unique gift allows these animals to detect the angle of *dip* (the angle between the magnetic field and the earth's surface) and regional variation in the field's strength. Magnetoreception helps them form a magnetic map, giving these birds and animals a built-in GPS. One such bird, the Arctic tern, migrates over forty-four thousand miles each year from the North Pole to Antarctica. In a typical lifespan of thirty years, the tern will migrate 1.3 million miles. My mother, who was raised on a farm in Sinton on the Texas Gulf Coast, will tell you she once had a pet parrot that was blown away in a hurricane only to return weeks later, featherless and on foot. These miraculous instincts and accurate senses of direction of these birds and animals still confuse modern scientific reasoning. God's miracles are amongst us, and many of us are unaware.

What is considered a miracle? According to Wikipedia, a miracle is "an event that is inexplicable by natural or scientific laws and accordingly gets attributed to some supernatural or preternatural cause." A biblical perspective, as quoted from *Smith's Bible Dictionary*, defines a miracle as "a plain and manifest exercise by a man, or by God at the call of a man, of those powers which belong only to the Creator and Lord of nature." For purposes of this writing, I would consider a miracle as a sign or an event that is only possible through God's power for a given reason, possibly to encourage us or make us constantly aware of His presence and majesty.

Have you ever given much thought on how we are healed? This can be a physical, spiritual, or emotional healing. As a two-time cancer survivor, I am constantly amazed at how God uses technology, coupled with the wisdom given to doctors and scientists, to save lives and help us heal. I think we sometimes take for granted where this healing comes from. Spiritual healing is not to be confused with the televangelist type of faith healing. Spiritual healing comes from experiencing a true relationship with God that purifies our hearts, minds, and souls. Because we live in an imperfect and fallen world, we are all destined to feel emotional pain through grief, despair, loneliness, depression, anxiety, and more. God can help heal us through this pain by relying on Him for answers and through the aid of professional Christian counseling. God is healing us today through everyday miracles, very much like He did two thousand years ago when Jesus laid hands on the sick and lame.

On New Year's Eve 1962, my baby sister, Leigh Ann (age two), was accidentally run over by a car in the driveway of our home. It was a miracle that a four-thousand-pound car could run over a thirty-pound child and she could survive. Sometimes bad things happen to good families. In this case, a tragic accident changed the entire course of the Mayo family, but many generations would benefit from it. That dreaded evening, my thirty-year-old father, Bill Mayo, promised God that if He allowed his baby daughter to live, he would begin taking his family to church. My dad followed up on his promise, and he saw to it that we were in church every Sunday after that. Our small family of four joined Grace Bible Church in Dallas in 1963. Not only was Leigh Ann healed physically, but the entire family healed spiritually. Each of us individually accepted Christ as our personal savior at Grace Bible. I am thankful my father took the lead in our family to get us to church. If my dad hadn't have taken that bold step, I can only wonder how easily led astray the family's faith could have been. My sister, Leigh Ann, was never expected to have children after the accident, but God is good, and her now adult children, Ashleigh and Mayo, and their families are Christ followers today. Another miracle.

One of my favorite pastimes is to observe my wonderful wife, Barbara, read books and tell stories to our grandchildren sitting in her lap. There is a special bond and love present that exists between sharing those tales. Stories help develop the imagination in the young and old. Stories can also provide hope, especially when life seems difficult or mundane. Jesus showed this same love to His disciples by sharing parables, relatable stories to help us realize our purpose in life and explain why He came to Earth in human form as our personal savior. As I was a small child attending church services, I would often come home not remembering much about the sermon, but I would always remember the stories shared at the pulpit. I could relate to the stories told and then visualize how I could make them applicable in my own spiritual walk.

In this book, I have attempted to recount factual accounts of miracles and signs performed by Jesus in the gospel of John, Messianic prophesies within the Old Testament—later fulfilled by Jesus in the New Testament—and modern-day miracles. Though we cannot see God's miracles in the same way today, He is still healing physically, spiritually, and emotionally in a very large way. As was well stated by Mike McKendrick, whose story is featured later in this book, "God is still in the miracle business." When Jesus walked this earth two thousand years ago, He healed instantaneously. Even today, He can still heal us spiritually in the same way. He heals us physically and emotionally more often over time, testing our faith. The New Testament, Old Testament, and modern-day stories have not been embellished, as I have recorded only factual events. As the no-nonsense cop Joe Friday, known for his '60s radio and TV program *Dragnet*, would say each week, "Just the facts, ma'am."

The aim for my book is very straightforward—Jesus performed miracles and signs so that we may believe Jesus is our Messiah, our Savior, the Son of God, and by believing, we would have eternal life through Him. As described in John 20:30–31, "Jesus performed many other signs in the presence of his disciples, which are not recorded in this book. But these are written that you may believe that Jesus is the Messiah, the Son of God, and that by believing you may have life in His name."

I have written this book as a Christian who is 100 percent certain of my eternal destiny in Heaven—not because of my ministry, not because I am basically a good person, not because I was baptized or have written a book about God's work. I am certain because of my belief in His free gift, my faith in God, and my personal relationship with Christ that He indwells in me daily through His Holy Spirit. At the young age of eight, I recognized I was a sinner and asked God to forgive me of my past, current, and future sins, no matter how horrible. At that very moment, the Holy Spirit entered my life forever. I trusted He forgave me because I believe the promises He made in the scriptures of the Bible. Sadly, I realize not everyone shares the same beliefs, which is why I felt called to share these miracle stories. As believers, God has called us through The Great Commission (Matt. 28:16–20) to share with others how He can live in our lives here on Earth and in Heaven.

Life as a believer is a journey. God promises peaks and valleys in our lives with a very good ending. It wasn't until 2013, when I began an in-depth Bible study, that I began to have a clearer understanding of what the sanctification process of a Christian looks like. Our family went through some tremendous trials. In 2008, my father died of cancer. In 2009, my sister had a near-drowning incident that left her body so severely damaged she died in 2010. Then in 2012, I was diagnosed with the same, aggressive cancer that took my father. Following this forty-eight-month trial period, I realized my days on Earth are numbered and that before I get to Heaven, I want to know God better. Through Bible study, leadership, prison ministry, and involvement with my church, I began to dive deeper into what purpose He has called me to do and gain a deeper understanding of sanctification. If I had a cure for cancer, why would I keep that a secret? I feel the same way about the keys to salvation. They should not be hidden. At my father's funeral in August 2008, several men testified that Dad had approached many of his friends later in his life and had a sincere conversation about their faith. He would sometimes invite his pastor, Andy Wileman, to join him to visit his buddies because he cared about their eternal well-being. Several of his friends accepted Christ due to Dad's bold witnessing. My father was a people person, and today he is still experiencing this same joy with some of his family and fellow Christ followers in his new dwelling in Heaven. He left a great legacy that I choose to follow.

The four gospels—Matthew, Mark, Luke, and John—record at least forty-two miracles performed by Christ. This count excludes His greatest miracle, when Jesus was resurrected from the grave, as had been prophesied. This single event changed the course of our world forever. It gave us hope of good over evil and opportunity of eternal salvation through our election. The resurrection is written and recorded in all four gospels. Following His resurrection, Jesus appeared numerous times before His disciples, Mary Magdalene, strangers traveling on a road, and large groups of people over a forty-day period prior to His ascension into Heaven. This book contains eight of those miracles as recorded in the gospel of John.

In the short thirty-three years Jesus was on Earth, He fulfilled over three hundred prophecies that were written by the prophets in the Old Testament. For the purposes of this book, I have provided eight of these prophecies recorded in the Old Testament with cross-references of when and where they were fulfilled during Jesus's time on Earth. The mathematical probability of one person fulfilling the top forty-eight prophecies in his lifetime is 1 in $10^{157}$. These odds are equivalent to winning twenty-two lotteries in a row. Not coincidental events.

The last portion of this book contains some of my life experiences that have been seared into my memory. I have observed miracles that have taken place around me and my family, as well as stories from those I have befriended and are credible due to their faith. I also added a favorite story told by the late Reverend Billy Graham. I can attest these are very reliable sources. I can only imagine how many pages a book would be if all Christians, past and present, collectively brought forth all their stories telling how God had divinely intervened in everyday life.

SECTION ONE

# Messianic Prophecies Fulfilled in the New Testament

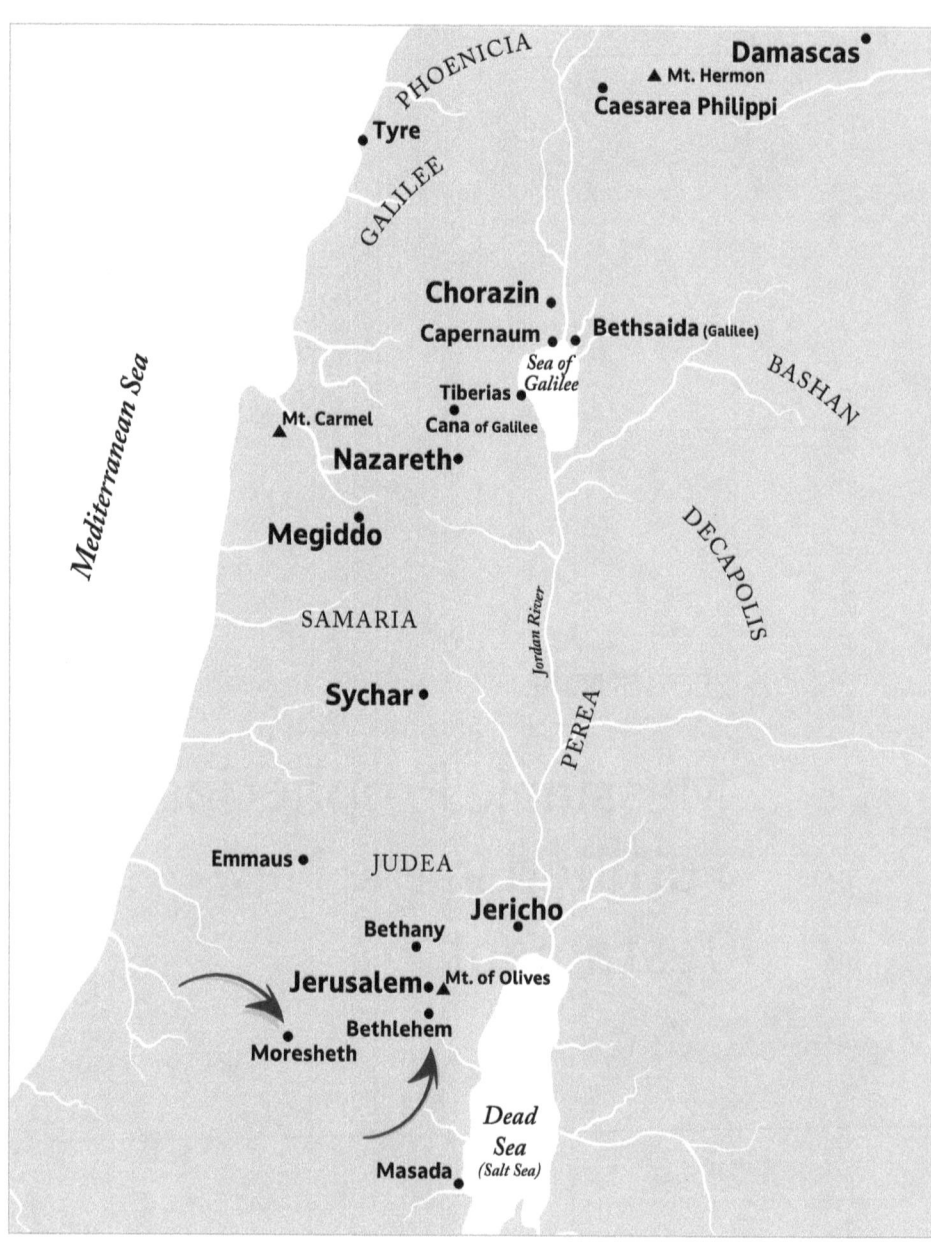

## CHAPTER 1
# *Born in Bethlehem*

| | |
|---|---|
| PROPHECY: | **Christ Would Be Born in Bethlehem** |
| PROPHET: | Micah |
| TIME OF PROPHECY: | 742–687 BC |
| LOCATION: | Moresheth (Gath)—20 miles SW of Jerusalem |

SCRIPTURE: Micah 5:1–4

> Marshal your troops now, city of troops,
> for a siege is laid against us.
> They will strike Israel's ruler
> on the cheek with a rod.
>
> "But you, Bethlehem Ephrathah,
> though you are small among the clans of Judah,
> out of you will come for me
> one who will be ruler over Israel,
> whose origins are from of old, from ancient times."
>
> Therefore Israel will be abandoned
> until the time when she who is in labor bears a son,
> and the rest of his brothers return

to join the Israelites.

He will stand and shepherd his flock

in the strength of the Lord,

in the majesty of the name of the Lord his God.

---

**DESCRIPTION OF PROPHECY:** Micah accurately predicted hundreds of years before Christ's birth in Bethlehem, in a district of Ephrathah, that our Ruler will reign over Israel, whose origins are from of old and ancient times. Jesus was from the lineage of King David, who was also born and raised in Bethlehem. Jesus, whose "origins are from ancient times" because He was alive and always existed, came to Earth as a man—yet God.

| | |
|---|---|
| **TIME PROPHECY WAS FULFILLED:** | 6/5 BC |
| **WITNESSES:** | God and His angels; Mary, mother of Jesus; Joseph, Mary's husband; Magi from the East (came later). Tradition is that there were three magi due to three gifts and were men of high position from the area of Parthia, near the site of ancient Babylon. |
| **LOCATION:** | Bethlehem |

**SCRIPTURE FULFILLED:** Matthew 2:1–2

After Jesus was born in Bethlehem in Judea, during the time of King Herod, Magi from the east came to Jerusalem and asked, "Where is the one who has been born king of the Jews? We saw his star when it rose and have come to worship him."

CHAPTER 2

# *Born of a Virgin*

| | |
|---|---|
| PROPHECY: | **The Messiah Is to Be Born of a Virgin** |
| PROPHET: | Isaiah |
| TIME OF PROPHECY: | 700 BC |
| LOCATION: | Jerusalem |

| | |
|---|---|
| SCRIPTURE: | Isaiah 7:14 |

Therefore the Lord himself will give you a sign: The virgin will conceive and give birth to a son, and will call him Immanuel.

DESCRIPTION OF PROPHECY: The prophet Isaiah was told of a sign by God that a son would be conceived from a virgin, and they would call Him Immanuel. Seven hundred years later, an angel appeared to Joseph in a dream and told him to take Mary as his wife and that she was with child conceived by the Holy Spirit.

| | |
|---|---|
| TIME PROPHECY WAS FULFILLED: | 5/4 BC |
| WITNESSES: | Joseph; an angel of God (through a dream) |

LOCATION: Bethlehem

SCRIPTURE FULFILLED: Matthew 1:18–25

This is how the birth of Jesus the Messiah came about: His mother Mary was pledged to be married to Joseph, but before they came together, she was found to be pregnant through the Holy Spirit. Because Joseph her husband was faithful to the law, and yet did not want to expose her to public disgrace, he had in mind to divorce her quietly.

But after he had considered this, an angel of the Lord appeared to him in a dream and said, "Joseph son of David, do not be afraid to take Mary home as your wife, because what is conceived in her is from the Holy Spirit. She will give birth to a son, and you are to give him the name Jesus, because he will save his people from their sins."

All this took place to fulfill what the Lord had said through the prophet: "The virgin will conceive and give birth to a son, and they will call him Immanuel" (which means "God with us").

When Joseph woke up, he did what the angel of the Lord had commanded him and took Mary home as his wife. But he did not consummate their marriage until she gave birth to a son. And he gave him the name Jesus.

CHAPTER 3

# *Riding on a Donkey*

| | |
|---|---|
| PROPHECY: | **The Messiah Is to Enter Jerusalem Riding on a Donkey in Triumph** |
| PROPHET: | Zechariah |
| TIME OF PROPHECY: | 480 BC |
| LOCATION: | Jerusalem |

SCRIPTURE:   Zechariah 9:9

> Rejoice greatly, Daughter Zion!
> Shout, Daughter Jerusalem!
> See, your king comes to you,
> righteous and victorious,
> lowly and riding on a donkey,
> on a colt, the foal of a donkey.

**DESCRIPTION OF PROPHECY:** The prophet Zechariah predicted five hundred years earlier that, prior to Jesus Christ's crucifixion and resurrection from the grave, He would ride victoriously into Jerusalem on a young donkey and the people would praise Him. When Jesus entered Jerusalem on a donkey's colt, he affirmed messianic royalty as well as his humility. The donkey symbolizes the peace Christ brings to humanity. This donkey had never been ridden; however, it carried the entire world's burdens on its back. When Christ returns, He will be on a warhorse, not a donkey; He will be mighty, not meek; He will return as a lion, not a lamb; and He will wear the crown of all crowns, not the crown of thorns.

TIME PROPHECY WAS FULFILLED:   AD 30
WITNESSES:   Jesus's disciples; a large group of people attending Passover: Feast of Unleavened Bread
LOCATION:   Bethphage (The Mount of Olives)

SCRIPTURE FULFILLED: Matthew 21:1–9

As they approached Jerusalem and came up to Bethphage on the Mount of Olives, Jesus sent two disciples, saying to them, "Go to the village ahead of you, and at once you will find a donkey tied there, with her colt by her. Untie them and bring them to me. If anyone says anything to you, say that the Lord needs them, and he will send them right away."

This took place to fulfill what was spoken through the prophet:

"Say to Daughter Zion,

'See, your king comes to you,
gentle and riding on a donkey,
and on a colt, the foal of a donkey.' "

The disciples went and did as Jesus had instructed them. They brought the donkey and the colt and placed their cloaks on them for Jesus to sit on. A very large crowd spread their cloaks on the road, while others cut branches from the trees and spread them on the road. The crowds that went ahead of Him and those that followed shouted,

"Hosanna to the Son of David!"
"Blessed is he who comes in the name of the Lord!"
"Hosanna in the highest heaven!"

CHAPTER 4

# *Betrayed for Thirty Pieces of Silver*

| | |
|---|---|
| **PROPHECY:** | **Jesus Would Be Betrayed for Thirty Pieces of Silver** |
| **PROPHET:** | Zechariah |
| **TIME OF PROPHECY:** | 480 BC |
| **LOCATION:** | Jerusalem |
| **SCRIPTURE:** | Zechariah 11:11–13 |

It was revoked on that day, and so the oppressed of the flock who were watching me knew it was the word of the Lord.

I told them, "If you think it best, give me my pay; but if not, keep it." So they paid me thirty pieces of silver.

And the Lord said to me, "Throw it to the potter"—the handsome price at which they valued me! So I took the thirty pieces of silver and threw them to the potter at the house of the Lord.

**DESCRIPTION OF PROPHECY:** Prior to Jesus's death and resurrection, He was betrayed by one of His followers, Judas Iscariot, for thirty pieces of silver. Judas informed the religious leaders that Jesus was located in the Garden of Gethsemane, accompanied by Peter, James, and John. In Zechariah, God instructed him to shepherd a flock of sheep being fattened for slaughter. The flock represents the Israelites who were feeding on their own greed and evil desires until they were ripe for God's judgment. To pay only thirty pieces of silver was an insult. It was the same price paid for a slave gored by an ox. Thirty pieces of silver was the exact amount paid to Judas. Overcome with guilt, Judas threw the thirty pieces of silver back to the chief priests and hung himself. They picked it up and used the money to buy the potter's field as a burial place for foreigners.

TIME PROPHECY WAS FULFILLED:   AD 30
WITNESSES:   Judas; chief priests; elders
LOCATION:   Jerusalem, Garden of Gethsemane

SCRIPTURE FULFILLED: Matthew 26:14–16; Matthew 27:3–8

> Then one of the Twelve—the one called Judas Iscariot—went to the chief priests and asked, "What are you willing to give me if I deliver him over to you?" So they counted out for him thirty pieces of silver. From then on Judas watched for an opportunity to hand him over (Matt. 26:14–16).

When Judas, who had betrayed him, saw that Jesus was condemned, he was seized with remorse and returned the thirty pieces of silver to the chief priests and the elders. "I have sinned," he said, "for I have betrayed innocent blood."

"What is that to us?" they replied. "That's your responsibility."

So Judas threw the money into the temple and left. Then he went away and hanged himself.

The chief priests picked up the coins and said, "It is against the law to put this into the treasury, since it is blood money." So they decided to use the money to buy the potter's field as a burial place for foreigners. That is why it has been called the Field of Blood to this day (Matt. 27:3–8).

CHAPTER 5

# *An Offering for Our Sins*

| | |
|---|---|
| PROPHECY: | **Jesus Would Die as an Offering for Our Sins** |
| PROPHET: | Isaiah |
| TIME OF PROPHECY: | 700 BC |
| LOCATION: | Jerusalem |

SCRIPTURE:   Isaiah 53:10–12

> Yet it was the Lord's will to crush him and cause him to suffer,
> and though the Lord makes his life an offering for sin,
> he will see his offspring and prolong his days,
> and the will of the Lord will prosper in his hand.
> After he has suffered,
> he will see the light of life and be satisfied;
> by his knowledge my righteous servant will justify many,
> and he will bear their inequities.
> Therefore I will give him a portion among the great,
> and he will divide the spoils with the strong,
> because he poured out his life unto death,

and was numbered with the transgressors.

For he bore the sin of many,

and made intercession for the transgressors.

---

**DESCRIPTION OF PROPHECY:** In the book of Isaiah, it is mentioned five times that the Lord's righteous servant would carry our sins for us. We cannot be part of God's Kingdom if marked with sin; therefore, the perfect Lamb of God, God's Son Jesus, took my sin and yours to the cross. This was the ultimate sacrifice to pave the way for followers of Christ to be accepted into His Kingdom upon our physical death here on Earth.

**TIME PROPHECY WAS FULFILLED:** AD 30

**WITNESSES:** Salome; Mary Magdalene; Mary, the mother of James and Joseph; two thieves on the cross (one was repentant); Simon of Cyrene (carried the cross); a centurion; Roman soldiers and numerous unnamed Jews and Gentiles; John (other disciples not mentioned)

**LOCATION:** Golgotha

---

**SCRIPTURE FULFILLED:** 1 Peter 2:24; Romans 5:6–8; 2 Corinthians 5:21

"He himself bore our sins" in his body on the cross, so that we might die to sins and live for righteousness; "by his wounds you have been healed" (1 Peter 2:24).

You see, at just the right time, when we were still powerless, Christ died for the ungodly. Very rarely will anyone die for a righteous person, though for a good person someone might possibly dare to die. But God demonstrates his own love for us in this: While we were still sinners, Christ died for us (Rom. 5:6–8).

God made him who had no sin to be sin for us, so that in him we might become the righteousness of God (2 Cor. 5:21).

CHAPTER 6

# *Death by Crucifixion*

| | |
|---|---|
| PROPHECY: | **The Messiah Is to Die by Crucifixion** |
| PROPHET: | David |
| TIME OF PROPHECY: | 1000–970 BC |
| LOCATION: | Bashan (east of the Sea of Galilee) |

| | |
|---|---|
| SCRIPTURE: | Psalm 22:14–18 |

I am poured out like water,
and all my bones are out of joint.
My heart has turned to wax;
it has melted within me.
My mouth is dried up like a potsherd,
and my tongue sticks to the roof of my mouth;
you lay me in the dust of death.

Dogs surround me,
a pack of villains encircles me;
they pierce my hands and my feet.
All my bones are on display;
people stare and gloat over me.
They divide my clothes among them
and cast lots for my garment.

DESCRIPTION OF PROPHECY: David made nineteen prophetic references to Christ in the book of Psalms that were later fulfilled in seven different books of the New Testament. When this prayer was written, David was suffering from rejection by his friends and going through a great trial. David knew God could lead him out of despair. He was writing an accurate description of the suffering Christ would endure on the cross one thousand years later. David would later gain victory over this trial, as Christ did when He was resurrected.

TIME PROPHECY WAS FULFILLED:     AD 30

WITNESSES:     Salome; Mary Magdalene; Mary, the mother of James and Joseph; two thieves on the cross (one was repentant); Simon of Cyrene (carried the cross); a centurion; Roman soldiers and numerous unnamed Jews and Gentiles; John (other disciples not mentioned)

LOCATION:     Golgotha

SCRIPTURE FULFILLED: Matthew 27:31, 35; Mark 15:20, 25

After they had mocked him, they took off the robe and put his own clothes on him. Then they led him away to crucify him. [ ... ] When they had crucified him, they divided up his clothes by casting lots (Matt. 27:31, 35).

And when they had mocked him, they took off the purple robe and put his own clothes on him. Then they led him out to crucify him. [ ... ] It was nine in the morning when they crucified him (Mark 15:20, 25).

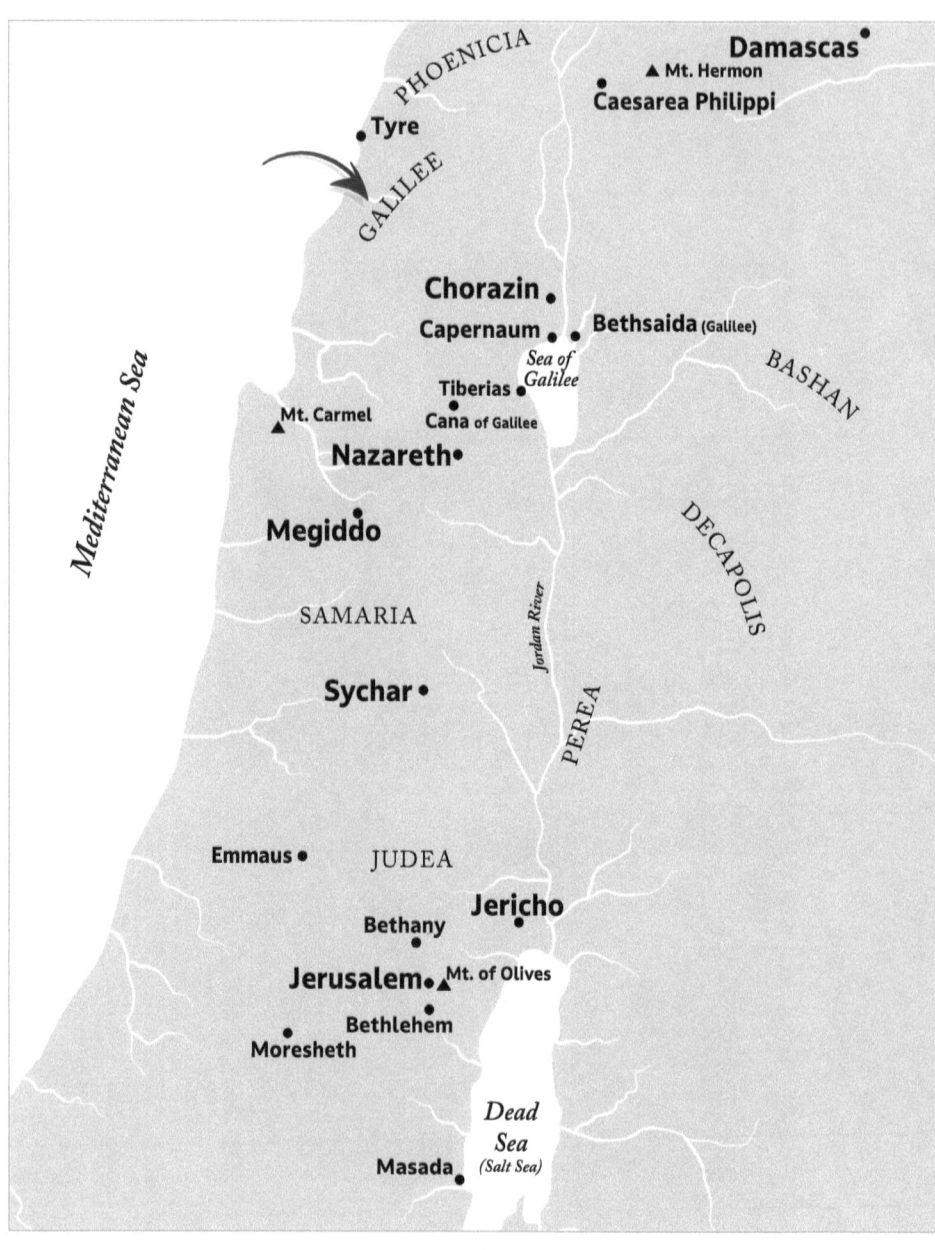

CHAPTER 7
# Jesus Foretold of His Death and Resurrection

| | |
|---|---|
| PROPHECY: | **Jesus Told His Disciples He Would Be Killed and Raised on the Third Day** |
| PROPHET: | Jesus Christ |
| TIME OF PROPHECY: | Within three years prior to Christ's death (AD 27) |
| LOCATION: | Galilee |
| SCRIPTURE: | Matthew 16:21; Mark 8:31; Luke 9:21–22 |

From that time on Jesus began to explain to his disciples that he must go to Jerusalem and suffer many things at the hands of the elders, the chief priests and the teachers of the law, and that he must be killed and on the third day be raised to life (Matt. 16:21).

He then began to teach them that the Son of Man must suffer many things and be rejected by the elders, the chief priests and the teachers of the law, and that he must be killed and after three days rise again (Mark 8:31).

Jesus strictly warned them not to tell this to anyone.

And he said, "The Son of Man must suffer many things and be rejected by the elders, the chief priests and the teachers of the law, and he must be killed and on the third day be raised to life" (Luke 9:21–22).

---

DESCRIPTION OF PROPHECY: Jesus predicted His own death three times (also in Matt. 17:22–23; 20:18) and, most importantly, His own resurrection. At the time, the disciples had a hard time understanding because they had preconceived notions about what the Messiah should do. The Jewish people, who were oppressed by the Romans, expected their king to overthrow their Roman enemies and were disappointed when Jesus came in love, not hate. They were hoping for a military coup led by Jesus. Instead, Jesus defeated a greater enemy (sin) by dying on the cross and rising from the dead. The Bible tells us that one day He will rule over the heavens and the earth with great majesty, and every person and creature will bow before Him.

John, the only disciple who witnessed Jesus's death, described in detail what Jesus went through that dark day. Crucifixion on the cross carried out by the Roman soldiers was a horrific and inhumane death. After being savagely whipped all morning, spikes were pounded into His hands and feet, and a crown of thorns was forced onto His scalp. There was a small platform on the cross that allowed Jesus and the other two being crucified with Him to slightly raise up by pushing against it with their feet, avoiding suffocation and collapse of the lungs. After the skies were darkened by God, the soldiers were ordered to break the legs of those being executed to accelerate their death. The soldiers broke the legs of the two criminals; however, Jesus was spared because He was already dead. Instead, they pierced His side with a spear, and blood and water were released. This was another fulfillment of the prophecy:

1. It was prophesied in Exodus 12:46 by Moses that, as a part of the Passover tradition, the bones of the unblemished sacrificial lamb should not be broken.
2. It was prophesied in Zechariah 12:10 that "they would look on me, the one they have pierced…"

John has also prophesied the second coming of Christ in Revelation 1:7: " 'Look, he is coming with the clouds,' and 'every eye will see him, even those who pierced him…' " All sinners, not just the Roman soldiers, pierced His side and are responsible for His death. Those who have rejected or neglected Him and those who believe in Him will all witness this second coming.

**TIME PROPHECY WAS FULFILLED:** AD 30

**WITNESSES:** (Crucifixion) Mary, mother of Jesus; Mary Magdalene; Mary's sister; John; Salome; a centurion; Simon of Cyrene; chief priests; scribes and elders; two thieves on a cross.

|  | (Resurrection) Mary Magdalene; Mary, mother of James; Salome; two believers traveling on the road to Emmaus (one was Cleopas); Simon Peter; John; (and then later) the disciples |
|---|---|
| **LOCATION:** | Golgotha (crucifixion); garden tomb (resurrection) |

**SCRIPTURE FULFILLED:** John 19:16–20:9 (See also Matthew 26:1–28:20; Mark 15:21–16:20; Luke 23:13–24:35)

Finally Pilate handed him over to them to be crucified.

So the soldiers took charge of Jesus. Carrying his own cross, he went out to the place of the Skull (which in Aramaic is called Golgotha). There they crucified him, and with him two others—one on each side and Jesus in the middle.

Pilate had a notice prepared and fastened to the cross. It read: JESUS OF NAZARETH, THE KING OF THE JEWS.

Many of the Jews read this sign, for the place where Jesus was crucified was near the city, and the sign was written in Aramaic, Latin and Greek. The chief priests of the Jews protested to Pilate, "Do not write 'The King of the Jews,' but that this man claimed to be king of the Jews."

Pilate answered, "What I have written, I have written."

When the soldiers crucified Jesus, they took his clothes, dividing them into four shares, one for each of them, with the undergarment remaining. This garment was seamless, woven in one piece from top to bottom.

"Let's not tear it," they said to one another. "Let's decide by lot who will get it."

This happened that the scripture might be fulfilled that said,

"They divided my clothes among them and cast lots for my garment."

So this is what the soldiers did.

Near the cross of Jesus stood his mother, his mother's sister, Mary the wife of Clopas, and Mary Magdalene. When Jesus saw his mother there, and the disciple whom he loved standing nearby, he said to her, "Woman, here is your son," and to the disciple, "Here is your mother." From that time on, this disciple took her into his home.

Later, knowing that everything had now been finished, and so that Scripture would be fulfilled, Jesus said, "I am thirsty." A jar of wine vinegar was there, so they soaked a sponge in it, put the sponge on a stalk of the hyssop plant, and lifted it to Jesus' lips. When he had received the drink, Jesus said, "It is finished." With that, he bowed his head and gave up his spirit.

Now it was the day of Preparation, and the next day was to be a special Sabbath. Because the Jewish leaders did not want the bodies left on the crosses during the Sabbath, they asked Pilate to have the legs broken and bodies taken down. The soldiers therefore came and broke the legs of the first man who had been crucified with Jesus, and then those of the other. But when they came to Jesus and found that he was already dead, they did not break his legs. Instead, one of the soldiers pierced Jesus' side with a spear, bringing a sudden flow of blood and water. The man who saw it has given testimony, and his testimony is true. He knows that he tells the truth, and he testifies so that you also may believe. These things happened so that the scripture would be fulfilled: "Not one of his bones will be broken," and, as another scripture says, "They will look on the one they have pierced."

Later, Joseph of Arimathea asked Pilate for the body of Jesus. Now Joseph was a disciple of Jesus, but secretly because he feared the Jewish leaders. With Pilate's permission, he came and took the body away. He was accompanied by Nicodemus, the man who earlier had visited Jesus at night. Nicodemus brought a mixture of myrrh and aloes, about seventy-five pounds. Taking Jesus' body, the two of them wrapped it, with the spices, in strips of linen. This was in accordance with Jewish burial customs.

At the place where Jesus was crucified, there was a garden, and in the garden a new tomb, in which no one had ever been laid. Because it was the Jewish day of Preparation and since the tomb was nearby, they laid Jesus there.

**The Resurrection**

Early on the first day of the week, while it was still dark, Mary Magdalene went to the tomb and saw that the stone had been removed from the entrance. So she came running to Simon Peter and the other disciple, the one Jesus loved, and said, "They have taken the Lord out of the tomb, and we don't know where they have put him!"

So Peter and the other disciple started for the tomb. Both were running, but the other disciple outran Peter and reached the tomb first. He bent over and looked in at the strips of linen lying there but did not go in. Then Simon Peter came along behind him and went straight into the tomb. He saw the strips of linen lying there, as well as the cloth that had been wrapped around Jesus' head. The cloth was still lying in its place, separate from the linen. Finally the other disciple, who had reached the tomb first, also went inside. He saw and believed. (They still did not understand from Scripture that Jesus had to rise from the dead.)

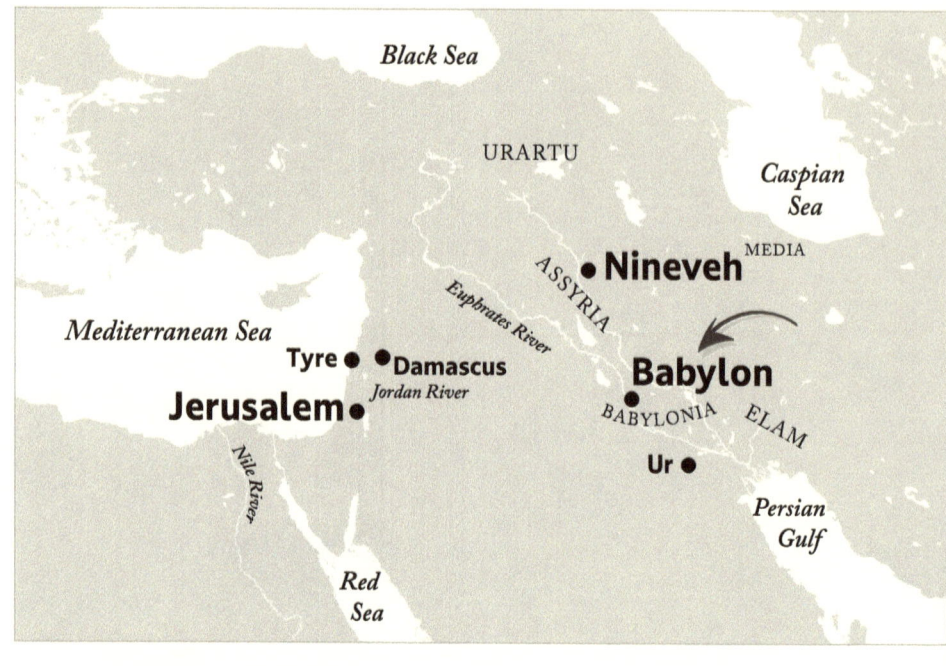

CHAPTER 8
# The Timing of His Death

| PROPHECY: | **Timing of Christ's Death** |
|---|---|
| PROPHET: | Daniel (as instructed by Gabriel) |
| TIME OF PROPHECY: | Approximately 536 BC |
| LOCATION: | Babylon (under rule of Nebuchadnezzar) |

| SCRIPTURE: | Daniel 9:24–27 |
|---|---|

"Seventy 'sevens' are decreed for your people and your holy city to finish transgression, to put an end to sin, to atone for wickedness, to bring in everlasting righteousness, to seal up vision and prophecy and to anoint the Most Holy Place.

"Know and understand this: From the time the word goes out to restore and rebuild Jerusalem until the Anointed One, the ruler, comes, there will be seven 'sevens' and sixty-two 'sevens.' It will be rebuilt with streets and a trench, but in times of trouble. After the sixty-two 'sevens,' the Anointed One will be put to death and will have nothing. The people of the ruler who will come will destroy the city and the sanctuary. The end will come like a flood: War will continue until the end, and desolations have been decreed. He will confirm a covenant with many

for one 'seven.' In the middle of the 'seven' he will put an end to sacrifice and offering. And at the temple he will set up an abomination that causes desolation, until the end that is decreed is poured out on him."

---

**DESCRIPTION OF PROPHECY:** Daniel prophesied the timing of Christ's death five hundred years prior to His birth:

- The Anointed One (Christ) will be put to death for our transgressions (sins) and to provide everlasting righteousness before the destruction of the temple in Jerusalem. He spoke of seventy "sevens"—seven-year periods or "weeks" of years. He foretold Christ would die after the sixty-ninth of these seven-year periods. Daniel then spoke of intense persecution, which will occur in the final forty-two months of the seven-year period, which we refer to as the Tribulation Period.

**TIME PROPHECY WAS FULFILLED:** The actual timing of the destruction of the temple "sixty-two sevens" can be interpreted three different ways:

1. During the destruction of the temple by the Romans (led by General Titus) in AD 70, when one million

Jews were killed.
2. When the temple was destroyed by Antiochus in AD 167. It was plundered in AD 169.
3. To be destroyed and the prophecy fulfilled at the time of the antichrist.

WITNESSES: The nation of Israel.

RECONSTRUCTION OF THE TEMPLE: Revelation 11:1–2

I was given a reed like a measuring rod and was told, "Go and measure the temple of God and the altar, with its worshipers. But exclude the outer court; do not measure it, because it has been given to the Gentiles. They will trample on the holy city for 42 months."

History reminds us that the temple was destroyed in AD 70. At the time of John's vision in AD 90, no temple remained in Jerusalem. Therefore, the command John receives must refer to a new temple, which would indicate construction of a new temple. There are two interpretations for those who will trample on the Holy City:

1. If the temple is to be rebuilt for the Jewish people, then this would refer to the Jews in Jerusalem. Or,
2. The temple may symbolize the church (all believ-

ers). John may have been instructed to measure the temple to show that God builds walls of protection around His people to spare them from spiritual destruction, and He has prepared a place for them in Heaven for those who remain faithful to Him.

RETURN OF CHRIST: Revelation 19:11–21

I saw heaven standing open and there before me was a white horse, whose rider is called Faithful and True. With justice he judges and wages war. His eyes are like blazing fire, and on his head are many crowns. He has a name written on him that no one knows but he himself. He is dressed in a robe dipped in blood, and his name is the Word of God. The armies of heaven were following him, riding on white horses and dressed in fine linen, white and clean. Coming out of his mouth is a sharp sword with which to strike down the nations. "He will rule them with an iron scepter." He treads the winepress of the fury of the wrath of God Almighty. On his robe and on his thigh he has this name written:

KING OF KINGS AND LORD OF LORDS

And I saw an angel standing in the sun, who cried in a loud voice to all the birds flying in midair, "Come, gather together for the great supper of God, so that you may eat the flesh of kings, generals, and the mighty, of horses and their riders, and the flesh of all people, free and slave, great and small."

Then I saw the beast and the kings of the earth and their armies gathered together to wage war against the rider on the horse and his army. But the beast was captured, and with it the false prophet who had performed the signs on its behalf. With these signs he had deluded those who had received the mark of the beast and worshiped its image. The two of them were thrown alive into the fiery lake of burning sulfur. The rest were killed with the sword coming out of the mouth of the rider on the horse, and all the birds gorged themselves on their flesh.

---

**TIME PROPHESIED AS CHRIST'S RETURN:** Jesus said it was not for us to know of the timing of His return.
**WITNESSES OF CHRIST'S RETURN:** Every eye of man, woman, child, and all the creatures of the earth will see Him.
**LOCATION:** (prophecy to be fulfilled) Mount of Olives, near Jerusalem

SECTION TWO

# Miracles by Jesus

CHAPTER 9

## *Water into Wine*

| | |
|---|---|
| MIRACLE: | **Jesus Turns Water into Wine** |
| TIME: | AD 26/27 |
| LOCATION: | Cana (Galilee) |
| SCRIPTURE: | John 2:1–11 |

On the third day a wedding took place at Cana in Galilee. Jesus' mother was there, and Jesus and his disciples had also been invited to the wedding. When the wine was gone, Jesus' mother said to him, "They have no more wine."

"Woman, why do you involve me?" Jesus replied. "My hour has not yet come."

His mother said to the servants, "Do whatever he tells you."

Nearby stood six stone water jars, the kind used by the Jews for ceremonial washing, each holding from twenty to thirty gallons.

Jesus said to the servants, "Fill the jars with water"; so they filled them to the brim.

Then he told them, "Now draw some out and take it to the master of the banquet."

They did so, and the master of the banquet tasted the water that had been turned into wine. He did not realize where it had come from, though the servants who had drawn the water knew. Then he called the bridegroom aside and said, "Everyone brings out the choice wine first and then the cheaper wine after the guests have had too much to drink; but you have saved the best till now."

What Jesus did here in Cana of Galilee was the first of the signs through which he revealed his glory; and his disciples believed in him.

---

WITNESSES: Mary, mother of Jesus; Nathaniel; Philip; Peter; Andrew; John; wedding guests

DESCRIPTION OF MIRACLE: A family friend of Mary's was having a wedding celebration. During this period, weddings typically lasted a week or more. Mary, possibly the wedding planner, scrambled to assist the family, as the wedding party was experiencing a shortage of wine for their guests. Running out of wine was a social taboo and humiliating to the bride and groom. Mary turns to her trusted and eldest son, Jesus, for a solution to the problem. Jesus's response: "Woman, why do you involve me?" The only other time Jesus referred to His mother as "woman" was at the cross; this was possibly because He wished to begin separating Himself as the son of Mary to her Heavenly Father. It is thought that Mary was not looking for a miracle, but simply hoping her son would help, as it is believed that her husband, Joseph, was most likely dead. Mary was bringing her problem to Jesus, just as Christ followers can bring their problems directly to Him. Jesus also replied, "My hour has not yet come." It was, in fact, the beginning of His ministry when others, besides His mother, Mary, began to realize he was sent by God (Mary knew at birth).

At the wedding, Jesus instructed the servants to fill the jars with water, draw some out, and take it to the master of the banquet. When the master of the banquet tasted the wine, he informed the bridegroom, "Everyone brings out the choice wine first and then the cheaper wine for the guests after they have had too much to drink, but you have saved the best until now." God brought the best, just as He wants the very best for our lives. When the disciples saw Jesus's miracle, they believed in Him. This miracle, the first of many (besides Mary conceiving the child as a virgin), showed His power over nature.

The powerful miracles and authoritative words by Jesus are revelations of His true identity so those would believe in Him.

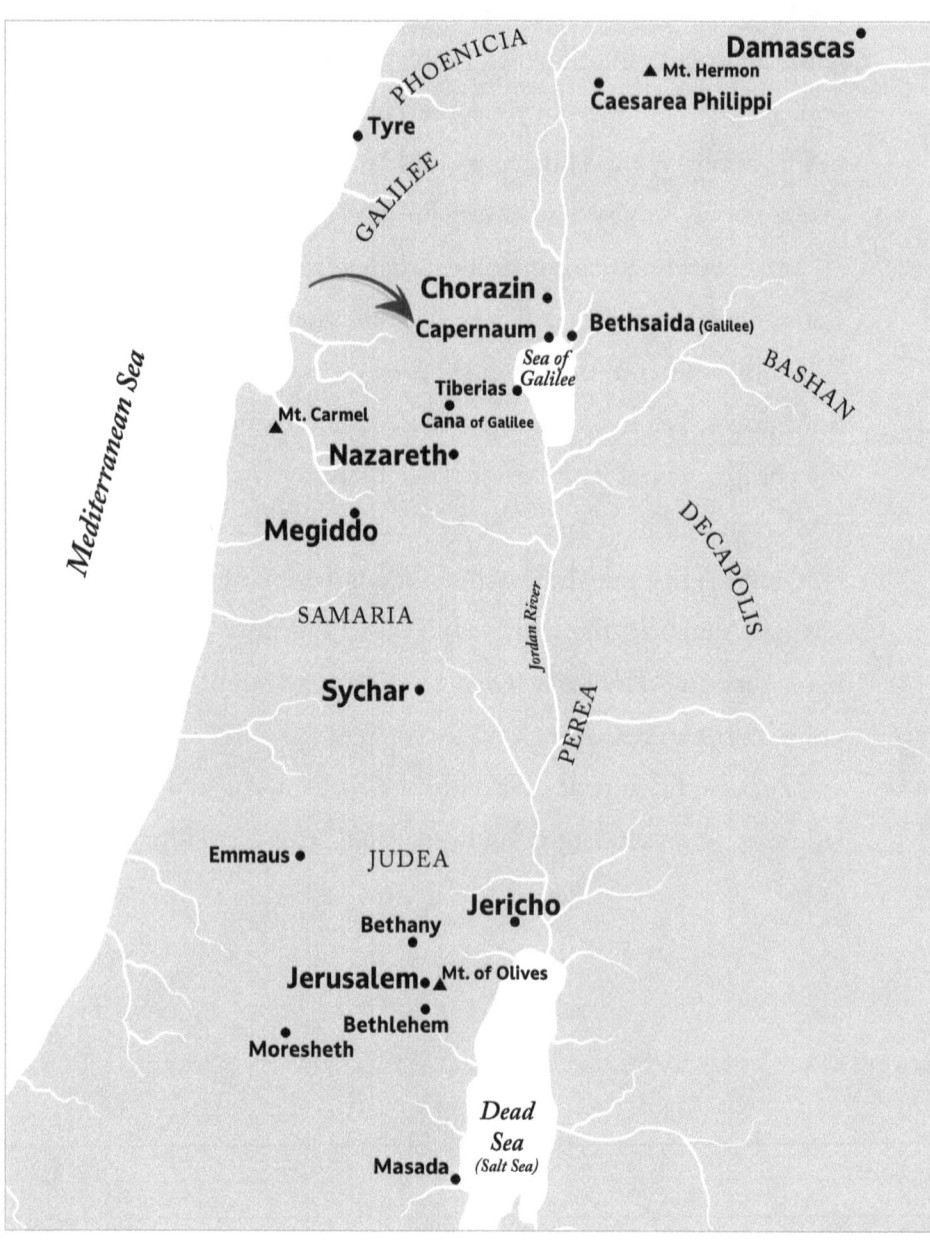

CHAPTER 10

# He Heals a Son

---

| | |
|---|---|
| MIRACLE: | **Jesus Heals a Government Official's Son** |
| TIME: | AD 26/27 |
| LOCATION: | Capernaum |

---

SCRIPTURE: John 4:46–54

Once more he visited Cana in Galilee, where he had turned the water into wine. And there was a certain royal official whose son lay sick at Capernaum. When this man heard that Jesus had arrived in Galilee from Judea, he went to him and begged him to come and heal his son, who was close to death.

"Unless you people see signs and wonders," Jesus told him, "you will never believe."

The royal official said, "Sir, come down before my child dies."

"Go," Jesus replied, "your son will live."

The man took Jesus at his word and departed. While he was still on the way, his servants met with the news that his boy was living. When he inquired as to the time his son got better, they said to him, "Yesterday, at one in the afternoon, the fever left him."

Then the father realized that this was the exact time at which Jesus had said to him, "Your son will live." So he and his whole household believed.

This was the second sign Jesus performed after coming from Judea to Galilee.

---

WITNESSES: Royal official (probably an officer in Herod's service); the official's servants

DESCRIPTION OF MIRACLE: A royal official approached Jesus's help as his son lay seriously ill. He was a loving and desperate dad who had lost hope for his son's recovery without a miracle. We have all witnessed this same scenario many times, experiencing others' grief over a loved one. I have seen this in my own family when my sister had her accident. The love that a father (or a mother) has for their own child is so strong it breaks our hearts when that child is in pain or suffering. The official begged Jesus to come and heal his son who was near death. Jesus's first response did seem harsh: "Unless you people see signs and wonders, you will never believe." His intent was to heal the boy, but first it was a greater priority to awaken the faith of the official. The "you" in Jesus's statement is plural, indicating He also spoke to the unbelieving people in His presence. Today, sometimes I begin to wonder what it takes for some of us to wake up spiritually. It's natural that we as parents worry when our children or grandchildren are sick or are in the hospital. Sometimes we allow fear to invade our minds. God's intent is to infiltrate our minds with a strong dependence on Him—not fear. He wants that dependency and relationship to be everlasting after the crisis is over. Jesus allowed the official to become shaken and dependent on Him to build his faith and trust in God. Praise God next time you or your loved one gets sick, taking comfort and knowing that He is the one who will miraculously heal us.

CHAPTER 11
# He Heals a Lame Man

| | |
|---|---|
| MIRACLE: | **Jesus Heals a Lame Man by a Pool** |
| TIME: | AD 26/27 |
| LOCATION: | Jerusalem (Bethesda) |
| SCRIPTURE: | John 5:1–15 |

Some time later, Jesus went up to Jerusalem for one of the Jewish festivals. Now there is in Jerusalem near the Sheep Gate a pool, which in Aramaic is called Bethesda and which is surrounded by five covered colonnades. Here a great number of disabled people used to lie—the blind, the lame, the paralyzed. One who was there had been an invalid for thirty-eight years. When Jesus saw him lying there and learned that he had been in this condition for a long time, he asked him, "Do you want to get well?"

"Sir," the invalid replied, "I have no one to help me into the pool when the water is stirred. While I am trying to get in, someone else goes down ahead of me."

Then Jesus said to him, "Get up! Pick up your mat and walk." At once the man was cured; he picked up his mat and walked.

The day on which this took place was a Sabbath,

and so the Jewish leaders said to the man who had been healed, "It is the Sabbath; the law forbids you to carry your mat."

But he replied, "The man who made me well said to me, 'Pick up your mat and walk.'"

So they asked him, "Who is this fellow who told you to pick it up and walk?"

The man who was healed had no idea who it was, for Jesus had slipped away into the crowd that was there.

Later Jesus found him at the temple and said to him, "See, you are well again. Stop sinning or something worse may happen to you." The man went away and told the Jewish leaders that it was Jesus who had made him well.

---

WITNESSES: Jesus's disciples; Jewish leaders; a great number of other invalids who were blind, lame, and paralyzed

DESCRIPTION OF MIRACLE: While Jesus was attending one of the Jewish festivals on the day of the Sabbath in Jerusalem (all Jewish males were required to attend the Festival of Passover and Unleavened Bread, the Festival of Weeks [also called Pentecost], and the Festival of Tabernacles in Jerusalem), he was led to the pool at Bethesda where He encountered a man who had been lame for thirty-eight years. Jesus asked him if he wanted to get well. The invalid made an excuse that whenever the water was stirred and he tried to get in, someone would always get in front of him. Jesus told him, "Get up! Pick up your mat and walk." The man was cured right then, and he obeyed Jesus's commandment by picking up his mat and walking.

Some of us may have experienced extended periods of doubt, uncertainty, and sickness or issues such as alcoholism, substance abuse, pornography, gambling, or social media addiction. Many of us tend to fall into a rut when we become too comfortable with our issues. My pastor has described this as some doing life with their feet set in concrete blocks. This can sometimes last for years, hindering God's intentions for our lives. Jesus did not want to hear the lame man's excuses but wanted him to act. When we lean on Him through prayer for wisdom, God can provide the right resources for us to be healed, such as Christian counseling, treatment centers, church recovery groups, and guidance from fellow believers.

When I was in my thirties, I was in a job situation where I felt trapped. Shortly after I began my new job, I knew the work environment did not parallel with my personal faith and ethical standards, but I was afraid if I moved companies again so soon, it would look poorly on my resume and I would not be attractive to a quality firm. At the time, we had two small children and had just bought a new home, doubling my mortgage payment. Even my father suggested I stick it out. I sought counsel from two very established Christian businessmen and a trusted associate pastor at my church. They all gave me the exact same, and very sound, advice to immediately leave the firm. After much prayer with my wife, Barbara, I resigned two days later and had the opportunity to share my testimony with my employer. I had two strong job offers within forty-eight hours. God had answered our prayers in a large way. I spent the next thirty years with two great employers and, as it turned out, had made a great career choice to move on. As with the lame man, Jesus was instructing me to "*get up* and pick up my mat." Thirty years later, I feel blessed and look back at this pivotal time in my life as one of the best decisions I have ever made.

CHAPTER 12

# *He Feeds Five Thousand*

| MIRACLE: | **Jesus Feeds Five Thousand** |
|---|---|
| TIME: | AD 29 |
| LOCATION: | Far north shore of the Sea of Galilee (Sea of Tiberias) |
| SCRIPTURE: | John 6:1–14 (also recorded in all four gospels) |

Some time after this, Jesus crossed to the far shore of the Sea of Galilee (that is, the Sea of Tiberias), and a great crowd of people followed him because they saw the signs he had performed by healing the sick. Then Jesus went up on a mountainside and sat down with his disciples. The Jewish Passover Festival was near.

When Jesus looked up and saw a great crowd coming toward him, he said to Philip, "Where shall we buy bread for these people to eat?" He asked this only to test him, for he already had in mind what he was going to do.

Philip answered him, "It would take more than a half year's wages to buy enough bread for each one to have a bite!"

Another of his disciples, Andrew, Simon Peter's brother, spoke up, "Here is a boy with five small barley loaves and two small fish, but how far will they go among so many?"

Jesus said, "Have the people sit down." There was plenty of grass in that place, and they sat down (about five thousand men were there). Jesus then took the loaves, gave thanks, and distributed to those who were seated as much as they wanted. He did the same with the fish.

When they all had enough to eat, he said to the disciples, "Gather the pieces that are left over. Let nothing be wasted." So they gathered them and filled twelve baskets with the pieces of the five barley loaves left over by those who had eaten.

After the people saw the sign Jesus performed, they began to say, "Surely this is the Prophet who is to come into the world."

---

WITNESSES: The disciples—the Bible specifically references Philip; Andrew (Simon Peter's brother); a young boy; five thousand men, plus women and children

DESCRIPTION OF MIRACLE: After healing the lame man, the Jewish religious leaders recognized Jesus's claim to deity and plotted to have Him killed. Due to the growing opposition in Jerusalem, Jesus left Capernaum with the disciples and fled to the hill country on the north shore of the Sea of Galilee. Word of the miracles performed had spread like wildfire, and the multitudes began to follow Jesus and the disciples, hoping to witness a miracle or to be healed. He was now approaching three years into His public ministry. At times, Jesus felt overwhelmed by the crowd but had a deep compassion for them. Jesus and the disciples recognized His followers had been traveling far from home and saw they needed food. Jesus challenged Philip, who was from nearby Bethsaida, with where they could buy food for the people. Jesus knew His intentions to feed the people all along, but He wanted to test his faith and provide an opportunity for Philip to recognize He could and would provide everything. Philip was shocked by His request because he knew it would take a half year's wages for everyone present to have a bite. Andrew saw a young boy who had five loaves of barley bread and two fish. The boy gave him all he had. Jesus then instructed the disciples to have the crowds sit down, and He took the loaves from the boy and passed them out amongst those seated. It is estimated that to feed fifteen thousand people (with the assumption each man had a spouse and one child), it would have taken at least five thousand pounds of food. The people ate as much food as they wanted and had plenty left over. There were twelve leftover baskets—one for each disciple.

God is not bound by logistics. This young boy entrusted his lunch to Jesus and His disciples, setting an example for us today what Jesus can do with our sacrificial giving. God then allowed this boy to witness His power. There are some circumstances during which we do not have the answers, but God is always in control. This day,

God showed up in a big way! After He fed the crowd, He gathered the leftover baskets, as He did not want the food to go to waste. God again provides us what we need. Jesus met the physical needs of the multitude to demonstrate His unlimited power and generous compassion. As was the case for Philip, God sometimes allows our situation to feel hopeless before His divine intervention.

CHAPTER 13

# *He Walks on Water*

---

| | |
|---|---|
| MIRACLE: | **Jesus Walks on the Water** |
| TIME: | AD 29 |
| LOCATION: | Sea of Galilee |

| | |
|---|---|
| SCRIPTURE: | John 6:16–21 (also recorded in Matthew & Mark) |

When evening came, his disciples went down to the lake, where they got into a boat and set off across the lake for Capernaum. By now it was dark, and Jesus had not yet joined them. A strong wind was blowing and the waters grew rough. When they had rowed about three or four miles, they saw Jesus approaching the boat, walking on the water; and they were frightened. But he said to them, "It is I; don't be afraid." Then they were willing to take him into the boat, and immediately the boat reached the shore where they were heading.

---

| | |
|---|---|
| WITNESSES: | The disciples |

**DESCRIPTION OF MIRACLE:** Following the feeding of the five thousand, Jesus tested His disciples' faith. While He hung back to pray with His Father, Jesus sent His disciples ahead to Capernaum across the Sea of Galilee by boat. The disciples encountered a frightening storm. Though there were several experienced fishermen aboard, they were afraid for their lives.

I've been caught on a lake in a storm while sailing a Hobie Cat, so I can relate well to the disciples here. One of my greatest fears is having my sixteen-foot aluminum mast struck by lightning, or being cast overboard and drowning in choppy waters. You tend to feel helpless as the turbulent winds toss the sailboat off course with no control of the sails and rudder. I have cruised on a small tour boat with my wife at precisely the exact location Jesus walked on the water in the Sea of Galilee. This freshwater lake is fed by the Jordan River to the north and sits almost seven hundred feet below sea level. The Sea of Galilee is surrounded by hills two thousand feet above sea level. At night, the changing temperature of air currents around and above the Sea of Galilee commonly produces violent storms, which can easily swamp a small boat. The disciples found themselves in a similar storm.

Sometimes life is not a straight-line course. God allows storms in our lives very much like what happened to His disciples. Because we live in an imperfect world, we will encounter storms, such as illness, loss of family members, marriage difficulty, loss of occupation or income, substance abuse, or catastrophic injury. These storms in life can either strengthen our relationship with God or, if we choose an alternative course, leave us adrift without Him.

Jesus had sent His disciples into this storm in the dark, allowing them to feel hopeless in their own power. After attempting to row to safety, they saw Jesus walking across the water to the boat, and they became transfixed on Him. He reminded them not to be afraid, boarded the boat, and calmed the sea.

At precisely the right time, Jesus was there for His disciples. He tends to show up when we need Him most. While facing difficult trials in my life, I have tried to fix things for myself and failed. When I remind myself (or someone like my spouse reminds me) that I am not the one in control, God is, I am overcome with goosebumps simply from knowing He is there. I am also reminded that He has *always* been there and, when I look back at all the answered—and sometimes unanswered—prayers, I know He has a genuine, loving concern for our best interests.

CHAPTER 14
# He Heals a Blind Man

| | |
|---|---|
| MIRACLE: | **Jesus Heals a Blind Man** |
| TIME: | AD 29 |
| LOCATION: | Siloam |

| | |
|---|---|
| SCRIPTURE: | John 9:1–41 |

As he went along, he saw a man blind from birth. His disciples asked him, "Rabbi, who sinned, this man or his parents, that he was born blind?"

"Neither this man nor his parents sinned," said Jesus, "but this happened so that the works of God might be displayed in him. As long as it is day, we must do the works of him who sent me. Night is coming, when no one can work. While I am in the world, I am the light of the world."

After saying this, he spit on the ground, made some mud with the saliva, and put it on the man's eyes. "Go," he told him, "wash in the pool of Siloam" (this word means "Sent"). So the man went and washed, and came home seeing.

His neighbors and those who had formerly seen him begging asked, "Isn't this the same man who used to sit and beg?" Some claimed that he was.

Others said, "No, he only looks like him."

But he himself insisted, "I am the man."

"How then were your eyes opened?" they asked.

He replied, "The man they call Jesus made some mud and put it on my eyes. He told me to go to Siloam and wash. So I went and washed, and then I could see."

"Where is this man?" they asked him.

"I don't know," he said.

They brought to the Pharisees the man who had been blind. Now the day on which Jesus had made the mud and opened the man's eyes was a Sabbath. Therefore the Pharisees also asked him how he had received his sight. "He put mud on my eyes," the man replied, "and I washed, and now I see."

Some of the Pharisees said, "This man is not from God, for he does not keep the Sabbath."

But others asked, "How can a sinner perform such signs?" So they were divided.

Then they turned again to the blind man, "What have you to say about him? It was your eyes he opened."

The man replied, "He is a prophet."

They still did not believe that he had been blind and had received his sight until they sent for the man's parents. "Is this your son?" they asked. "Is this the one you say was born blind? How is it that now he can see?"

"We know he is our son," the parents answered, "and we know he was born blind. But how can he see now, or who opened his eyes, we don't know. Ask him. He is of age; he will speak for himself." His parents said this because they were afraid of the Jewish leaders, who already had decided that anyone who acknowledged that Jesus was the Messiah would be put out of the synagogue. That is why his parents said, "He is of age; ask him."

A second time they summoned the man who had been blind. "Give glory to God by telling the truth," they said. "We know this man is a sinner."

He replied, "Whether he is a sinner or not, I don't know. One thing I do know. I was blind but now I see!"

Then they asked him, "What did he do to you? How did he open your eyes?"

He answered, "I have told you already and you did not listen. Why do you want to hear it again? Do you want to become his disciples too?"

Then they hurled insults at him and said, "You are this fellow's disciple! We are disciples of Moses! We know that God spoke to Moses, but as for this fellow, we don't even know where he comes from."

The man answered, "Now that is remarkable! You don't know where he comes from, yet he opened my eyes. We know that God does not listen to sinners. He listens to the godly person who does his will. Nobody has ever heard of opening the eyes of a man born blind. If this man were not from God, he could do nothing."

To this they replied, "You were steeped in sin at birth; how dare you lecture us!" And they threw him out.

Jesus heard that they had thrown him out, and when he found him, he said, "Do you believe in the Son of Man?"

"Who is he, sir?" the man asked. "Tell me so I may believe in him."

Jesus said, "You have now seen him; in fact, he is the one speaking with you."

Then the man said, "Lord, I believe," and he worshiped him.

Jesus said, "For judgment I have come into this world, so that the blind will see and those who see will become blind."

Some Pharisees who were with him heard him say this and asked, "What? Are we blind too?"

Jesus said, "If you were blind, you would not be guilty of sin; but now that you claim you can see, your guilt remains."

---

WITNESSES: The disciples; neighbors of the healed man; the healed man's parents

**DESCRIPTION OF MIRACLE:** There are three recorded incidents of Jesus healing the blind, which occurred in Jericho, Bethsaida, and Siloam. At Siloam, Jesus's disciples asked if a man was born blind because of his own sin or his parents' sin. Jesus answered, neither. He was born blind so that the works of God could be displayed. Here Jesus discounted generational sin. Jesus spat on the ground, put mud on the blind man's eyes, and instructed him to wash his eyes in the Pool of Siloam. Through God's miracle, the man began to see. The Pharisees attempted to discredit this miracle and threw the healed man out of the temple. But Jesus used the blind man's healing to make the world aware of spiritual blindness. In fact, we are all born spiritually blind. We are blind to God's truth until the Holy Spirit speaks to us individually, giving every one of us the vision and opportunity to accept Christ personally.

One of my favorite stories in the Bible is the story of Saul and how he later became Paul on the road to Damascus. After Jesus Christ's ascension to Heaven, Saul, a zealous Pharisee, went on a personal campaign to persecute the new Christians through jail time and execution. While on this road, he was confronted by Christ through a flash of light and a voice from Heaven. Saul was overcome and fell to the ground. Jesus asked Saul why he was persecuting Him. Christ physically blinded Saul and gave him instructions to go into the city of Damascus, where he would be told what to do next. Saul was left with no sight and did not eat for three days. Later, Jesus instructed a disciple, Ananias, in a vision to find Saul from Tarsus at the house of Judas on Straight Street. Ananias was fearful of Saul for the damage he had caused Christ through the persecution of His believers. But Christ said to Ananias, "Go! This man is my chosen instrument to proclaim my name to the Gentiles and their kings and to the people of Israel. I will show him how much he must suffer for my name" (Acts 9:15). Once Saul was located, Ananias was told by Christ to place his hands on him to restore his sight. After Ananias placed his hand on Saul, "scales fell from his eyes," and he could see once again (v. 18).

Saul, renamed Paul in Acts 13, could not only see with his eyes again, but now spiritually as well. God's intentions for his life were now clear. Paul went on to become Christ's greatest ambassador. An imperfect man, who once was responsible for killing Christians and attempting to dismantle the Christian faith, was now a transformed man with a strong passion to carry out Christ's commission. Paul went on to write fourteen books (fifteen if you include Hebrews) in the New Testament and, due to his faith, has won millions for Christ. The good news is scales continue to fall even today.

Historical records indicate Paul was martyred for Christ after the Christians were held responsible by the Roman Empire for the burning of Rome in AD 64.

CHAPTER 15
# He Raises Lazarus

| | |
|---|---|
| MIRACLE: | **Jesus Raises Lazarus from the Dead** |
| TIME: | AD 29 |
| LOCATION: | The village of Bethany (two miles east of Jerusalem on the road to Jericho) |

| | |
|---|---|
| SCRIPTURE: | John 11:1–44 |

Now a man named Lazarus was sick. He was from Bethany, the village of Mary and her sister Martha. (This Mary, whose brother Lazarus now lay sick, was the same one who poured perfume on the Lord and wiped his feet with her hair.) So the sisters sent word to Jesus, "Lord, the one you love is sick."

When he heard this, Jesus said, "This sickness will not end in death. No, it is for God's glory so that God's Son may be glorified through it." Now Jesus loved Martha and her sister and Lazarus. So when he heard that Lazarus was sick, he stayed where he was two more days, and then he said to his disciples, "Let us go back to Judea."

"But Rabbi," they said, "a short while ago the Jews there tried to stone you, and yet you are going back?"

Jesus answered, "Are there not twelve hours of daylight? Anyone who walks in the daytime will not stumble, for they see by this world's light. It is when a person walks at night that they stumble, for they have no light."

After he had said this, he went on to tell them, "Our friend Lazarus has fallen asleep; but I am going there to wake him up."

His disciples replied, "Lord, if he sleeps, he will get better." Jesus had been speaking of his death, but his disciples thought he meant natural sleep.

So then he told them plainly, "Lazarus is dead, and for your sake I am glad I was not there, so that you may believe. But let us go to him."

Then Thomas (also known as Didymus) said to the rest of the disciples, "Let us also go, that we may die with him."

On his arrival, Jesus found that Lazarus had already been in the tomb for four days. Now Bethany was less than two miles from Jerusalem, and many Jews had come to Martha and Mary to comfort them in the loss of their brother. When Martha heard that Jesus was coming, she went out to meet him, but Mary stayed at home.

"Lord," Martha said to Jesus, "if you had been here, my brother would not have died. But I know that even now God will give you whatever you ask."

Jesus said to her, "Your brother will rise again."

Martha answered, "I know he will rise again in the resurrection at the last day."

Jesus said to her, "I am the resurrection and the life. The one who believes in me will live, even though they die; and whoever lives by believing in me will never die. Do you believe this?"

"Yes, Lord," she replied, "I believe that you are the Messiah, the Son of God, who is to come into the world."

After she had said this, she went back and called her sister Mary aside. "The Teacher is here," she said, "and is asking for you." When Mary heard this, she got up quickly and went to him. Now Jesus had not yet entered the village, but was still at the place where Martha had met him. When the Jews who had been with Mary in the house, comforting her, noticed how quickly she got up and went out, they followed her, supposing she was going to the tomb to mourn there.

When Mary reached the place where Jesus was and saw him, she fell at his feet and said, "Lord, if you had been here, my brother would not have died."

When Jesus saw her weeping, and the Jews who had come along with her also weeping, he was deeply moved in spirit and troubled. "Where have you laid him?" he asked.

"Come and see, Lord," they replied.

Jesus wept.

Then the Jews said, "See how he loved him!"

But some of them said, "Could not he who opened the eyes of the blind man have kept this man from dying?"

Jesus, once more deeply moved, came to the tomb. It was a cave with a stone laid across the entrance. "Take away the stone," he said.

"But, Lord," said Martha, the sister of the dead man, "by this time there is a bad odor, for he has been there four days."

Then Jesus said, "Did I not tell you that if you believe, you will see the glory of God?"

So they took away the stone. Then Jesus looked up and said, "Father, I thank you that you have heard me. I knew that you always hear me, but I said this for the benefit of the people standing here, that they may believe that you sent me."

When he had said this, Jesus called in a loud voice, "Lazarus, come out!" The dead man came out, his hands and feet wrapped with strips of linen, and a cloth around his face.

Jesus said to them, "Take off the grave clothes and let him go."

---

WITNESSES: Mary (sister of Lazarus—same one that poured perfume on Jesus's feet and wiped them with her hair); Mary's sister Martha; the disciples; some Jewish friends of Lazarus's family

**DESCRIPTION OF MIRACLE:** Jesus had been preaching east of Judea in an area of Perea when He learned Lazarus was gravely ill. Jesus did not immediately leave for Bethany, much to the dismay of Lazarus's sisters, Mary and Martha, who knew that Jesus could have easily healed their brother before he died. Jesus intentionally delayed His trip by two days and said, "This sickness will not end in death. No, it is for God's glory so that God's Son may be glorified through it" (John 11:4).

God's timing is not necessarily our timing. We must trust God with this. Unexpected death always leaves a wake of unknown answers and grief, causing us to ask God why. He has His reasons that we will not know until we have the opportunity to ask Him personally.

Both Martha and Mary confronted Jesus when He finally arrived and asked Him why He didn't arrive earlier. Lazarus had been in the tomb for four days. "Lord, if you had been here, my brother would not have died," Martha said to Jesus (v. 21). Jesus comforted each of the siblings in separate ways. Despite her grieving emotions, Martha told Jesus she knew Lazarus would rise again in the resurrection on the last day. She knew the promises Christ had made for those who believe in Him and that our bodies would be resurrected at the time of His second coming. Jesus reassured her by responding in verse 25: "I am the resurrection and the life. The one who believes in me will live, even though they die; and whoever lives by believing in me will never die."

Mary had stayed back in her home with her friends who were attempting to comfort her. Martha informed Mary that Jesus was on His way, so she and her Jewish friends rushed to meet with Him. When Jesus greeted Mary, she fell to His feet weeping. Jesus saw how upset she was and was "deeply moved in spirit and troubled" (v. 33). Then Jesus wept (v. 35). Jesus was taken to Lazarus's tomb, instructed others to roll away the stone, and commanded Lazarus to come out. Miraculously, Lazarus came out of the tomb alive. He was still in his grave clothes, and Jesus instructed others to take them off. (It should be noted that though Lazarus was risen at this occasion in Bethany by Christ, his physical body died again later. As Christians, the instant our physical bodies die here on Earth, our spirit will immediately be with Christ—at the time of His second coming, our bodies will then rise.)

Christ raised Lazarus from the dead for several good reasons.

- In verse 41, He said, "Father, I thank you that you have heard me. I knew that you always hear me, but I said this for the benefit of the people standing here, that they may believe that you sent me." God wanted others in His presence to witness the power of God—so that they would believe. And God hears us when we call on Him. He may not answer immediately, for He has His own timing.
- In verse 28, Jesus asked for Mary. Jesus asks for us even when we avoid Him or attempt to hide. He wants to be a part of our daily lives.
- By Jesus weeping, He has shown us He is a compas-

sionate God. When we hurt, He also hurts with us. Very much like when our own children are hurt, we also feel their pain. Because we live in a broken world, we cannot escape pain from grief, sickness, disease, or hardship, but we can always call on Him for healing. He promises no more tears, sickness, or death in Heaven for those that believe. This is extremely comforting and gives us all hope.

- Jesus instructed those at the grave of Lazarus to take off his grave clothes. When we accept Christ as new believers, we clothe ourselves in righteousness as the Holy Spirit indwells us. The grave clothes are a symbol of our old self, which was tangled in sin and eternal death. As Christ followers, we adorn ourselves with the full armor of God so that we can withstand sin, temptation, and the forces of evil (Eph. 6:11–13). Spiritual warfare is very real. Satan continues to try and break down the moral fiber of good by attacking us individually, our children and the family unit, our schools, the media, our government, and our country.

Today is a good day to shed the grave clothes.

CHAPTER 16

# *Resurrection*

| | |
|---|---|
| MIRACLE: | **Jesus Is Resurrected** |
| TIME: | AD 30 |
| LOCATION: | Jerusalem (the garden tomb prepared by Joseph of Arimathea) |

| | |
|---|---|
| SCRIPTURE: | John 20:1–29 |

Early on the first day of the week, while it was still dark, Mary Magdalene went to the tomb and saw that the stone had been removed from the entrance. So she came running to Simon Peter and the other disciple, the one that Jesus loved, and said, "They have taken the Lord out of the tomb, and we don't know where they have put him!"

So Peter and the other disciple started for the tomb. Both were running, but the other disciple outran Peter and reached the tomb first. He bent over and looked in at the strips of linen lying there but did not go in. Then Simon Peter came along behind him and went straight into the tomb. He saw the strips of linen lying there, as well as the cloth that had been wrapped around Jesus's head. The cloth was still lying in its place, separate from the linen. Finally the other disciple, who had reached the tomb first, also went inside. He saw and believed. (They still did not understand from Scripture that Jesus had to rise from the dead.) Then the disciples went back to where they were staying.

Now Mary stood outside the tomb crying. As she wept, she bent over to look into the tomb and saw two angels in white, seated where Jesus's body had been, one at the head and the other at the foot.

They asked her, "Woman, why are you crying?"

"They have taken my Lord away," she said, "and I don't know where they have put him." At this, she turned around and saw Jesus standing there, but she did not realize that it was Jesus.

He asked her, "Woman, why are you crying? Who is it you are looking for?"

Thinking he was the gardener, she said, "Sir, if you have carried him away, tell me where you have put him, and I will get him."

Jesus said to her, "Mary."

She turned toward him and cried out in Aramaic, "Rabboni!" (which means "Teacher").

Jesus said, "Do not hold on to me, for I have not yet ascended to the Father. Go instead to my brothers and tell them, 'I am ascending to my Father and your Father, to my God and your God.'"

Mary Magdalene went to the disciples with the news: "I have seen the Lord!" And she told them that he had said these things to her.

On the evening of that first day of the week, when the disciples were together, with the doors locked for fear of the Jewish leaders, Jesus came and stood among them and said, "Peace be with you!" After he said this, he showed them his hands and his side. The disciples were overjoyed when they saw the Lord.

Again Jesus said, "Peace be with you! As the Father has sent me, I am sending you." And with that he breathed on them and said, "Receive the Holy Spirit. If you forgive anyone's sins, their sins are forgiven; if you do not forgive them, they are not forgiven."

Now Thomas (also known as Didymus), one of the Twelve, was not with the disciples when Jesus came. So the other disciples told him, "We have seen the Lord!"

But he said to them, "Unless I see the nail marks in his hands and put my finger where the nails were, and put my hand into his side, I will not believe."

A week later his disciples were in the house again, and Thomas was with them. Though the doors were locked, Jesus came and stood among them and said, "Peace be with you!" Then he said to Thomas, "Put your finger here; see my hands. Reach out your hand and put it into my side. Stop doubting and believe."

Thomas said to him, "My Lord and my God!"

> Then Jesus told him, "Because you have seen me, you have believed; blessed are those who have not seen and yet have believed."

---

**WITNESSES:** Mary Magdalene; Mary, the mother of James; Salome; Joanna; the disciples (seven times); Cleopas and Simon (two believers traveling on the road); two angels of the Lord; guards at the tomb; a crowd of five hundred; Peter

**DESCRIPTION OF MIRACLE:** Of all the signs and miracles performed on Earth, the pinnacle of all miracles was when Jesus died on the cross and later resurrected on the third day, as was prophesied (by Jesus and several in the Old and New Testaments) and witnessed by many. Lazarus was also resurrected by Jesus, but he later died a natural death. Today, Jesus still lives because He ascended into Heaven forty days after His resurrection. This event is the single most important miracle ever. Believing in the resurrection is a life-changing decision that allows us to have eternal life, because Christ was the propitiation for all of our sins that were sacrificed on the cross that day. His resurrection guarantees us a spot in Heaven, should we elect to believe and follow Him.

Jesus promises: "Do not let your hearts be troubled. You believe in God; believe also in me. My Father's house has many rooms; if that were not so, would I have told you that I am going there to prepare a place for you? And if I go and prepare a place for you, I will come back and take you to be with me that you also may be where I am. You know the way to the place where I am going" (John 14:1–4).

Jesus's appearances after His resurrection:

| | |
|---|---|
| Mary Magdalene | Mark 16:9–11; John 20:11–18 |
| The other women at the tomb | Matthew 28:8–10 |
| Peter in Jerusalem | Luke 24:34; 1 Cor 15:5 |
| Two travelers on the road | Mark 16:12–13; Luke 24:13–35 |
| Ten disciples behind closed doors | Luke 24:36–43; John 20:26–31 |
| All the disciples, excluding Judas Iscariot | Mark 16:14; John 20:26–31; 1 Cor. 15:5 |
| Seven disciples while fishing | John 21:1–14 |
| Eleven disciples on the mountain | Matthew 28:16–20 |
| A crowd of 500 | 1 Cor. 15:6 |
| Jesus's brother James | 1 Cor. 15:7 |
| Those who watched Jesus ascend into Heaven | Luke 24:44–51; Acts 1:3–11 |

SECTION THREE

# Modern-Day Miracles

Map of Texas showing the cities of Amarillo, El Paso, Abilene, Jacksboro, Fort Worth, Coppell, Dallas, Tyler, Austin, San Antonio, Houston, and Corpus Christi. An arrow points to Austin.

CHAPTER 17

# *God's Provisions*

---

**Written by Ashleigh Allman (my niece)**

Reflections on her late mother, Leigh Ann Mayo Hawthorne (my sister), and her late grandfather, William L. "Bill" Mayo (my father)

---

| | |
|---|---|
| TIME OF MIRACLE: | **July 1, 2009** |
| LOCATION: | Austin, Texas |
| WITNESSES: | Ashleigh Whaley Allman; William Mayo Whaley (nephew); Bethany Whaley (W. Mayo's wife); Delle Mayo (my mother); Barbara Mayo (my wife); Hunter Mayo (my son); Joshua Mayo (my son); Hal Hawthorne (Leigh Ann's husband) |

## I

Taking care of family was the most important thing to Poppy (what we called my grandfather Bill Mayo), and he did it well. "Let's have a talk," he'd say, and it would usually have to do with my future. What seeds am I planting today to grow fruit in the future? That sort of thing. When he was diagnosed with cancer, spiritual matters became paramount. He wanted to know his family would be joining him in Heaven. In the summer of 2008, months before his death, he kept talking about this book he read called *90 Minutes in Heaven* by Don Piper. He had been gifting the book to some loved ones, but I was finishing my last semester of college and, selfishly, didn't want to think about the reality of death before I had to. I put the book on the shelf, and the cancer took him from us on August 18, 2008.

Two months after Poppy's death, I was working my first job out of college and feeling a bit lost. On a whim—or out of a subconscious desperation for answers—I grabbed *90 Minutes in Heaven* off the shelf and started reading. I was in complete awe of the book's description of Heaven. It spoke of how the angels' voices sound like all the music of the earth is playing at once and in total harmony, how colors unseen on Earth permeate the space, and, most importantly, how the author was greeted by a celestial welcoming committee led by his grandfather. Love beyond measure was the theme in Heaven. The book made me cry, not only for Poppy, but for the beauty and love that awaits those who know the Lord.

I called my brother to come visit me the day after finishing the book. I couldn't wait to tell him about it and gave him the book to read for himself. We talked about the book, Poppy, and how a near-death experience can be a true gift to many who struggle with doubt and fear of death. The miraculous nature of this life God gives us is a comfort and a blessing for those that believe, as well as a faith builder. After a few hours, my brother left my apartment. I walked to the bathroom, turned on the shower, and was about to step in when my cell phone started ringing from my bedroom.

It was about twelve thirty in the morning. No one calls me at that hour. I ran to catch it, and panic set in briefly. The screen read "Dee & Poppy," a name reserved for my grandparents' landline in Dallas. My precious grandmother, Dee, is usually asleep by nine thirty every night. If she is calling at twelve thirty in the morning, there is a problem. I just missed the call and hurriedly called back to see what she needed. I called two or three times, but she never answered. I went to bed and awoke the next morning highly concerned, so I called my mom. "Dee is in Austin with me," she said.

I don't know how a call was made from an empty house to my cell phone, but to this day, I still have a strong feeling Poppy called me that night to let me know he was happy I had read the book and shared it with my brother.

II

When Poppy died, my mom, Leigh Ann, was devastated. She told me she wouldn't last a year without her dad, and truly, she didn't. On June 30, 2009, she spent the evening at a friend's home in Austin. In the early morning hours of the next day, my twenty-fourth birthday, she was left alone in the hot tub while her friend went inside for an unknown reason. It's unclear what happened from there, but she was found at the bottom of the pool and pulled out unconscious by her friend and her friend's teenage daughter. When the paramedics arrived, they noted that no one was giving her CPR, and they estimated she had been without oxygen for fifteen to thirty minutes. Nothing would ever be the same for my mom and our family.

On that warm sunny morning, when I finally got to see her, she was in an induced coma and not moving. She remained that way for about a week. I'll never forget seeing her like that—still, quiet, just lying there with her perfectly pink manicured toes, like she was sleeping. Tears burst from my eyes as I told her to hang on, professing my love for her like I had never in my life. That entire day is now a core memory. I rushed outside the hospital doors to the side of the building where no one could see me, pointed my face at the sky, and screamed at God. "Save her! It's not her time, and she cannot go like this. Please, please, please, God, heal my mom." It was 100 percent clear she was in God's hands now and the future was unknown.

When she finally woke from her coma, her bright blue eyes were a geyser of tears, and she cried, and she cried, and she cried. There was so much crying. She was talking, which felt like a miracle to me, and I thought maybe she was going to survive this. But God had other plans for my mom. She could only talk, blink, smile, and cry, but was unable to move from the neck down. For the next seventeen months, she did not regain any more abilities, and her body deteriorated in a horrible way until she met her maker on November 15, 2010.

One of the first things Mom told us when she awoke from her coma was that she had seen Poppy in the pool. She'd had a conversation with him. It was very emotional for her, and she would cry for Poppy and wanted him there next to her. She had difficulty articulating why he had been in the pool with her and what they spoke about. However, over the course of a few days, it became clear to my family and me that Poppy showed up at her time of need, young looking, and eager to speak with her. He told her he was there to help, but that her timing was not right.

Her timing was *so* not right. First, she was forty-eight years young. Second, the last time I saw my mom before her near-drowning, we had one of the biggest arguments we had ever had. I will not put the details on this page, but the last time I saw her, she had been in her nightgown, sitting in her kitchen, waiting to talk to me the next morning after our fight. It was mid-June 2009. I didn't even look at her and rolled my suitcase out the door. I guess the message I was trying to send her was that I didn't need her anymore, but the truth was that I needed her so much. Several weeks later, on the eve of her drowning, she called me, and we did make amends. We had made plans to meet the next day for my birthday. I now wish I had dropped everything and rushed to her. It's something I think about often. We truly do not know how quickly life can change.

I don't like to speculate why God allows certain things to happen the way they do. After all, Proverbs 3:5–6 is the Mayo verse: "Trust in the LORD with all your heart and lean not on your own understanding; in all your ways submit to him, and he will make your paths straight." I'd like to think that God would not allow for that to have been the last time I saw my mother, that He knew I needed to hug and kiss her and care for her and tell her that no one had ever done more for me, and that there were no limits to my love for her. I'd like to think that my brother also needed to see her and speak to her and tell her how much he loved her. The amount of people who came to see my mom in those first few months in the hospital was absolutely overwhelming. My brother and I were not the only ones that needed to love on her, even just one last time. Again, I don't know why God allowed these things to happen, but I know for sure that He was close by the whole time my mom was in the hospital.

God was there the moment she drowned because He sent my mother's most beloved to her to comfort her in her trauma, to reassure her of her future. He was there as people filled the room with smiles and tears, talking and laughing at all the Leigh Ann stories, and there were plenty of those. He was there during the many months in which Dee and I took daily shifts sitting with my mom while she suffered immensely in a dozen different hospital rooms. His promises never left our hearts. As Psalm 34:18 says, "The LORD is near to the brokenhearted and saves the crushed in spirit."

In the mausoleum where the earthly bodies of Poppy and my mom lay to rest, there is a stained-glass window with a Bible verse that says, "The LORD is good, a strong hold in the day of trouble; and he knoweth them that trust in him" (Nahum 1:7, KJV). I find it a fitting verse to be displayed next to the tombs of those two Mayos. Without my stronghold, I would have been filled with despair over what happened to my mom. Some days I did feel despair, and still do, but God brought us all into His arms as our refuge, and He still does. That is a truth that will never leave my heart. I will never forget my refuge during those trying days.

Our lives on Earth are temporary, and the miracles our Lord performs remind me that our permanent home is with Him in deep love and joy. When I hear about near-death experiences and stories of Heaven, it is no surprise to me anymore, for we are separated from our Lord by a sheer veil, which will one day be ripped away. I can't wait to stand in His full glory, and seeing those two Mayos again will certainly be a beautiful occasion, but I will wait because God's timing is His and His alone.

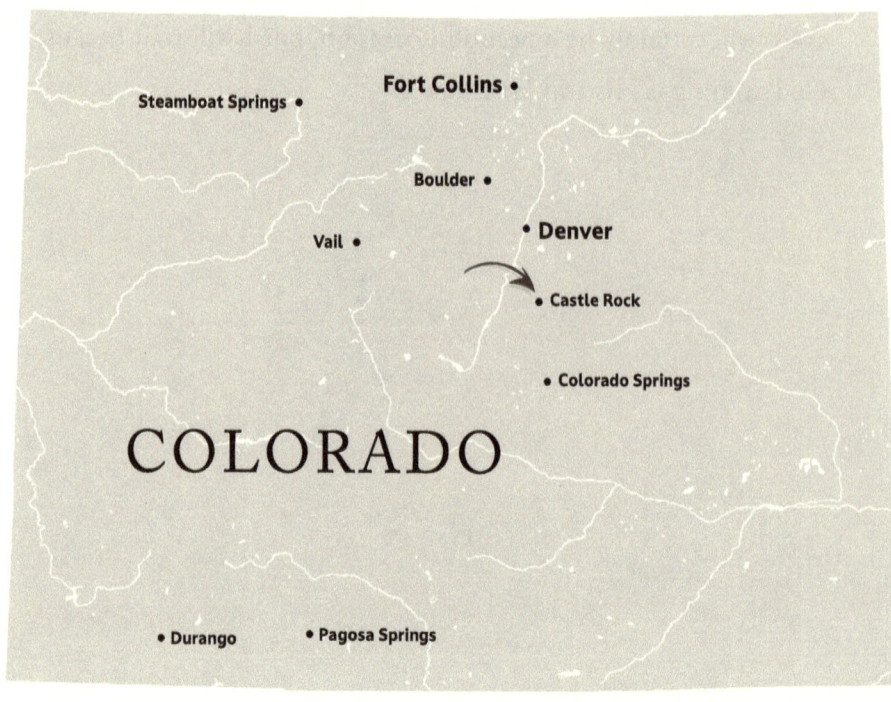

## CHAPTER 18
# *The Long Awakening*

---

| | |
|---|---|
| TIME OF MIRACLE: | **August 30, 2002** |
| LOCATION: | Castle Rock, Colorado |
| WITNESSES: | Tim O'Connor (a friend of mine); Tim and Lindsey's children—Jacquelyn, Claire, Allison, Collin, and Caroline (a newborn) |

Lindsey and Tim O'Connor had their fifth child on August 30, 2002. Their newborn baby, Caroline Aileen O'Connor, was brought into this world as a beautiful, healthy girl. But Lindsey experienced complications in childbirth and had to lay in a medically induced coma for the first forty-seven days of her baby's life. From day one, it was Tim, his four children, and their family friends who cared for baby Caroline while Lindsey was in the hospital. Her long, courageous journey of physical and emotional recovery began with the strength found through her faith in God and with the help of her devoted husband, children, and close friends. Her story has been a tremendous inspiration for many to carry on despite the most difficult circumstances life sometimes brings us. In Lindsey's book *The Long Awakening*, she shares the entire story of the second half of her life that she had almost missed.

Tim, Lindsey, and I met at Stephen F. Austin State University in Nacogdoches, Texas. Tim and I were freshmen in 1977, and Lindsey began attending two years after that. Tim and I pledged a fraternity together (Phi Delta Theta), and he became a very close, trustworthy friend of mine. Tim is a fun guy and could make everyone laugh, even during the long, challenging pledgeship "events." He never succumbed to the pressure the older fraternity members laid on him, despite how hard they tried. It wasn't disrespect; Tim carries a lot of self-confidence, and he just didn't let things bother him. He is six four and played football for SFA his freshman year. He could be a tough guy if he was pushed, but I've never seen him lose his temper. Tim's humor and laugh are contagious, and no matter how tough the circumstances, he can always make the room a little brighter.

After college, Tim and Lindsey married in the Houston area. I was in their wedding, and then Tim was in my wedding. I took my girlfriend (and future wife), Barbara, to their wedding in Spring, Texas. On the night of Tim and Lindsey's wedding rehearsal, the electricity went out in the church due to a storm, and the entire ceremony had to be illuminated by candlelight. Despite the circumstances, the entire wedding was magnificent and very intimate. Everyone who witnessed their vows knew they were a perfect match and felt confident they would live the rest of their days together. (Little did they know how important those unconditional marriage vows would be. They would be put to the test twenty years later.) With new job opportunities, we all moved out of Houston. The Mayos moved to Dallas, and the O'Connors eventually moved to Denver.

Over the next fifteen to twenty years, the economy began to improve and life was good. Most of our friends had begun to be fruitful and multiply. Some of us began to realize Tim's multiplication indices were slightly higher than the rest of us. After four children, they had their baby caboose nine years later, intentionally! As was the plan, at age forty, Lindsey would have her fifth child, Caroline. After she was born, the family and friends would take pictures, then Lindsey and baby would come home from the hospital after just a few days. Tim would spend part of the week at home, then head back to work, as was customary in those pre-paternity leave days. He would file another dependent on his income taxes and maybe purchase a larger dining table for his enlarged family. That was the plan.

1 Peter 4:12 says: "Dear friends, do not be surprised at the fiery ordeal that has come on you to test you, as though something strange were happening to you."

As some of us have started the 2020 decade as senior citizens, I have begun to realize if we live long enough, most of us will not dodge the bullet of these fiery trials. Peter was trying to prepare us for the trials in life that would rock our boat. Beginning in August 2003, the O'Connors' metaphorical boat was in a terrible storm for many days and months. At times, Tim and Lindsey may have thought their rocking boat would capsize and sink.

Lindsey, Tim, and their family went through one of life's toughest trials. Lindsey suffered unimaginable, near-fatal blood loss following the complications of their youngest's delivery. That awful night, Lindsey underwent two surgeries, and code white was called on more than one occasion. Much to Tim's surprise, the hospital called in the chaplain, and the nurse advised Tim to notify next of kin. Tim was told if they turned off the ventilator, she would die. Lindsey was initially diagnosed by the doctors with issues stemming from massive blood loss, oxygen deprivation, and "some manner of brain and lung injury," but they didn't know why. Tim learned sometime later that Lindsey had acute respiratory distress syndrome (ARDS), a life-threatening lung injury where the alveoli fill with fluid and the lungs can no longer get oxygen to the blood. ARDS patients can experience a life of numerous complications, including organ failure, with a high mortality rate.

The doctors didn't have a whole lot of answers. Tim waited patiently, praying constantly for forty-seven days for Lindsey to wake up. Even if she regained consciousness, Tim had no idea how damaged Lindsey's brain and body would be from the oxygen deprivation. The O'Connors' family, friends, church, and community were all in shock when they heard the news of Lindsey's grave condition. The phone lines lit up every night for weeks, though there weren't any encouraging signs of improvement from Tim's regular reports coming out of Denver. In 2003, we were all in our early forties and were supposed to be invincible. None of our friends had died this early in life, especially with young children. How could Tim possibly take care of five children by himself? He had a great job, but how could he care for this baby, watch the kids after school, see that they were properly clothed and fed, and all the rest that went with child care all by himself? What if Lindsey was disabled mentally and physically? What kind of physical and financial challenges would that bring? I cannot even imagine what was going on in Tim's mind when all his questions were left unanswered. It was more than any one man could handle.

Before Lindsey's unconsciousness began, she had been able to hold her baby for what seemed like five minutes.

Lindsey then remained in an induced coma for what felt like an eternity. While in a coma, doctors tried to wean her off her medications, attempting to wake her, but her vital signs would drop dramatically.

She was on a ventilator and feeding tube, hanging onto life with the best equipment medical science could provide.

Meanwhile, Tim had a baby at home, four hungry children, and a crop in the field. But Lindsey was no Lucille. She never gave up—she is a fighter. Tim did his very best to manage the situation while working all day, visiting the hospital in late afternoons to be at Lindsey's bedside, and then returning home very late each night.

His oldest daughter, Jacquelyn, had just started her freshman year in college, but she decided to drop her classes to help with her newborn sister and other siblings. Jacquelyn was there every day to encourage her siblings and wipe away their tears as they worried about losing their mom. She prepared the meals for her family, leaving dinner covered in foil on the kitchen table for her dad when he returned home from the hospital late at night. At eighteen, Jacquelyn stepped into the maternal role for her four siblings.

Tim would periodically send out text messages to update his

friends and community who were praying for Lindsey. His first message was as follows:

> All, first let me say that words cannot express deeply enough the gratitude, blessing, and comfort I and my children have in knowing that so many are praying for us. THANK YOU ALL.
>
> On the medical front, on Friday, the medical staff made two attempts during the day to move Lindsey up to the room for the MRI test they want to do on her brain. In order to do that, it requires that she be disconnected from her vent machine and manually vented for the trip to the MRI room. Both times resulted in a drop in vital signs—primarily oxygenation—so that the nurses were forced to cancel the test. On the second attempt, she made it to just outside the door of the MRI room before they stopped and returned her to ICU.
>
> The pulmonologist is also pursuing more information that would explain the decline in Lindsey's lung function over the course of the last week.
>
> Last evening, I took Caroline up to be with Lindsey—laid the baby on her chest again. During this time, Lindsey tried to open her eyes—Praise our God!!!! We plan to repeat this "treatment" for Lindsey and Caroline as often as is practical.
>
> God bless you All, Tim

A couple of weeks into the coma, I received a very tough telephone call from Tim. It was a voice that I had never heard before from my buddy of twenty-six years. It was a voice and words that no one ever wants to hear. We wept together. I still vividly remember our conversation twenty-two years ago when he couldn't get all his words out entirely, but he didn't have to; I knew where this conversation was going. I stopped Tim mid-sentence and prayed with him. When I got off the phone, I shared with Barbara that we probably ought to begin clearing our calendars for an upcoming memorial service. I called some of my other college friends—Matt, Walt, Bart, Scott, John, and Vince—learning they were also getting the same idea from Tim. Barbara and I prayed that night together, confident that our God was still in the miracle business.

Not long after this, Tim faced an agonizing decision with significant risk: Would he allow the doctors to wake Lindsey from her medically induced coma once she was stable enough and attempt to transfer her to Craig Hospital, a nationally renowned facility for spinal cord and brain injuries? Craig had been reported in the *US News and World Report* to be one of the ten best hospitals in its field. There was new hope, but at a pre-admittance evaluation, a Craig nurse cautiously prepared Tim for the condition Lindsey could most likely be in once she was awakened. If she made it through the transfer, and the brain trauma was not as severe as originally believed, Lindsey would still need intensive occupational therapy for an extended time. That would mean she would be relearning how to talk, walk, dress herself, feed herself, et cetera. Those resounding wedding vows "in sickness and in health" I am sure came to the forefront of Tim's mind.

In her book, Lindsey perfectly describes Tim's emotions and feelings after making the monumental, life-threatening decision to allow her awakening:

> He stood up and walked over to the bulletin board next to the glass doors and looked at the two pictures he'd hung—one taken hours before the birth, and one moments after. He looked at the smile he knew so well.
>
> A gritty resolve bubbled up, a strength from a depth he'd never known, from God, as real as the unseen wind that shakes autumn leaves loose every fall. It took him back to his belief and life motto, which had been tested near to the breaking point, shaken, but not broken, and had gotten him through these darkest of days.
>
> You play the hand you're dealt.
>
> You play it without false hope or despair, without comparing other people's hands, or questioning why you've got this hand, you just play it, as best you can, today, and the next day, and the day after that. If he could trust God to be good in a world that was not, if the end of this life is the beginning of another, and beliefs he held sacred in a God he held sacred could inform his decisions and withstand his worst moments, then he could play the hand he was dealt.

Which took him back to the words he'd written when my death was imminent. "It is my desire to let all of you know, that whether Lindsey comes home, or goes Home, glory to God."

He turned his back to the pictures on the bulletin board, away from what he most longed for, away from the expectations of how I might be, away from the images of what, who, I'd been, and walked to my bedside, kissing me as he often did, the me I was now, ready to keep playing his hand (2013, p. 209).

A love story tested to the core.

Just one week later, Tim called again, and this time spoke with a very hopeful tone. His voice was now in rally mode! He confidently explained to me his decision, despite the risk.

As it turned out, Tim had made the right decision. He had trusted God and heeded good counsel from the doctors and others. Lindsey had survived the transfer! She was awakened from her deep sleep of forty-seven days and would spend one hundred and seven days in the hospital, mostly in the ICU. Despite the great news that she had made the transfer, the doctor's initial report was that her brain was hurt "some," but Lindsey would later prove that she was able to regain all of her cognitive faculties! The trauma would continue though; there were many hard days and weeks that would prove she was definitely not out of the woods. In addition to ARDS, Lindsey still had to deal with a myriad of complications in her body, including respiratory issues, kidney failure, blood clots, multi-organ failure, coma-related sleep disorders, sleep apnea, anoxia, and more. In addition, she would suffer from post-traumatic stress disorder. According to Lindsey, PTSD did not settle in immediately but later haunted her for a long time. Tim was very patient with her long recovery and ecstatic to have her home under his roof where he could keep an eye on her around the clock.

Over many months, Lindsey gradually began to heal physically and emotionally, but life still continued to throw challenges her way.

Several years later, on one very nice sunny day, Lindsey and her daughter Jacquelyn drove into town for some casual shopping and necessary errands when Lindsey received a call from her son: "Caroline's fallen out of the window!"

"What window?" Lindsey asked.

"Her bedroom," he answered. Her bedroom was on the second floor over a full walk-out basement. Her child had just fallen three stories.

"Is she moving? Is she breathing?" Lindsey cried. Lindsey sped home at over 90 mph while Jacquelyn patiently explained to emergency dispatch on the cell phone which window she had fallen out of and where their home was located in the foothills.

Lindsey tried to calm herself. She could not allow two horrible accidents to happen on the same day, so she backed off the accelerator. Her emotions raced through her head, which was still trying to recover from her PTSD. She had no idea what to expect of her daughter's condition when she arrived. Would she find her little daughter dead after all they had been through? More than any mother can handle. Lindsey writes: "Only one thing matters now. I want this baby girl more than anything in my life. I want to love this girl, fully, more than anything in my life. And in an instant, I realize I do" (2013, p. 222). After a traumatic ambulance drive to the hospital, they were met by a large ER team. When the doctor's prognosis came: "I'm having a hard time finding anything wrong with her," tensions began to ease. Caroline spent a precautionary night in the pediatric ICU, then was released to go home the next day, bruised and shaken but okay. The seas have calmed again.

At one point during Lindsey's illness, sixty people had gathered in the basement of their church to pray for God's intervention on behalf of Lindsey as she suffered. Lindsey later found out through letters and emails that hundreds of friends, family, and strangers had also been praying for her. Lindsey's experience would show that miracles, like hers, do occur and the power of prayer is very real. I do believe God healed her because He was not done with her yet. Lindsey has a career she loves, a loving husband, five grown children, and now six grandchildren who want to spend the next few decades with her. She has a strong testimony and purpose that can be shared with many.

Some of us struggle with why God answers prayer for some and not for others. Lindsey was no exception. On this side of Heaven, I don't think there are any good answers, but God has all the answers. He has had the answers since the beginning. He has just chosen to allow this to be one of His mysteries for whatever reason, and I have chosen to accept that.

Years after her illness, Lindsey still wasn't clear on what she had learned or why she had been spared from her near-death experience, until a revelation one special evening…

Lindsey writes:

> One night, years after my experience, right after the Haiti earthquake devastated Port-au-Prince, I drove down I-25 in Denver, listening to a Colorado Public Radio interview. A man named James Gulley described how he had endured five days under the rubble of the Montana hotel that had collapsed in the quake. He'd been trapped in a five-foot-high space with five colleagues for five days until French rescuers heard them. He told of singing and prayer, darkness and hope, and pain; two of his colleagues did not survive the ordeal. I listened to his extraordinary tale, captivated. Then, there it was. The question. The interviewer asked him, "What did you learn?" It struck me that he was being asked this question when he had only been rescued a few days earlier. How much can we possibly understand the meaning of what may be a singular, unprecedented life event only days after experiencing it?
>
> He hesitated. I turned the radio up. Two seconds of silence, then this:
>
> "Well, I think it's easy to spout platitudes about 'Wow, God saved my life.' Well, He didn't save the lives of my

two colleagues. I can't answer theologically the question of why my life was spared and the lives of my friends were not spared. I can't answer the question of why the lives of thousands and thousands of Haitians have been lost. It's not about being favored. There's always a mystery there as to why one person is more fortunate than another. All one can do is say I have been given a gift. A new gift of life. And all I can do is use that gift in the best way possible. Not selfishly for myself but for the sake of other people. And… I will do it not only because I've gotten that life, but for the sake of those who didn't get that life as well."

Lindsey adds: "I listened to his astounding answer and wanted to pull over to the shoulder and weep. That's it. That's it, I thought—use the gift; offer it up, offer it out. Live well, live grateful, forever" (2013, pp. 230–31).

When Lindsey meets her Maker one day, I have no doubt some of His first words will be, "Lindsey, job well done."

---

Lindsey O'Connor is a longtime journalist; an author of five books, including her memoir *The Long Awakening*; and an audio producer. Her radio, podcast, and print works include *American Public Media, WHYY, The Texas Standard, The Washington Post, Rocky Mountain News, Pacific Content, Christianity Today, Writer's Digest,* and many others. She's a former broadcaster, has reported internationally, was a finalist for an Audie Award, a Fellow in the Entrepreneurial Journalism Creators Program at CUNY Craig Newmark Graduate School of Journalism, and is a member of the Association of Independents in Radio and Religion News Association. She also publishes *The Triple Thread* at lindseyoconnor.substack.com about meaning-rich living from the trifecta of journalism, story, and faith.

# Texas

- Amarillo
- Jacksboro
- Coppell
- Fort Worth
- Dallas
- Abilene
- Tyler
- El Paso
- Austin
- Houston
- San Antonio
- Corpus Christi

CHAPTER 19

# *Modern-Day Lazarus*

| | |
|---|---|
| TIME OF MIRACLE: | **January 2021** |
| LOCATION: | Fort Worth, Texas |
| WITNESSES: | Mike McKendrick; Lynn McKendrick (Mike's wife); Mark McKendrick (Mike's son); Caroline McKendrick (Mark's wife); Matt McKendrick (Mike's son); Courtney McKendrick (Matt's wife) |

The coronavirus, commonly known as Covid, was known to infect 704,753,890 people from 2020 to 2023. More than seven million would perish during this time. This dreaded virus changed our lives, shut down our economy, and impacted our families worldwide.

In 2023, we were studying John 11 in our international, nondenominational Bible study. One early Friday morning, one of our leaders stood up and with great emotion shared that his father was a "modern-day Lazarus." Mark McKendrick's father, Mike, fought Covid and survived to tell the miraculous story. God had already laid on my heart that He wanted me to write a book on His miracles. So, after cornering Mark following leadership class that morning, he shared with me how his dad had come through this ordeal and how his health had made a remarkable turn. Now, Mike and Mark's family were sharing the good news with others about his survival.

Their faith cemented my thoughts to carry forward with my book.

Mark arranged for his father, Mike McKendrick, and me to meet. Mike is a big guy, with fire in his eyes and a burning passion in his heart for God larger than life. Mike formerly played football for TCU in his hometown of Fort Worth and has always had a can-do attitude. I immediately picked up that failure is not in his vocabulary. Mike shared with me that even when hope seemed lost, God's provisions, prayer, and his family's faith pulled him through this health crisis. Just before his forty-fifth wedding anniversary at age sixty-seven, Mike tested positive for Covid on January 6, 2021. At this time in our history, Covid was at its peak, and all of the hospitals were already at full capacity. The virus dominated the national spotlight with daily worldwide reports stating that we were experiencing the worst health epidemic in modern history. Our doctors had no answers, our president had no answers, and vaccines were months away from availability. Just when things seemed hopeless, God stepped up, as He always does. He has the answers because He has a bigger plan.

The following is Mike's story as told by his son, Mark McKendrick:

> I'll preface by saying I know a lot of guys who have scars that are bigger than mine and have dealt with hardships bigger than what I am going to share. My purpose in sharing is to acknowledge what God has done for me and my family and what he is capable of doing for us.
>
> I'm going to talk about two things: the power of prayer and the power of God's plan.

### MY DAD

Before my dad, Mike, caught Covid, he would work out at five in the morning, play golf on the weekends, and had recently hit his first hole-in-one. Sixty-seven years old with no underlying health conditions.

In early January, he caught Covid. This was before vaccinations and when ERs were overflowing with patients, but it was manageable. He went to the doctor; they looked at his lungs; he went home.

The next night, he didn't get any sleep and felt like he was breathing through a straw. That morning, he was admitted to the Covid ICU with double pneumonia and got the last bed available.

My mom was instructed to quarantine. She was not allowed to visit my dad, and we were not allowed to be in physical contact with her for two weeks. My dad had his cell phone and was able to send and receive text messages from his hospital bed with updates.

However, his condition began to spiral quickly.

The ICU doctor said my dad's Covid condition was among the worst they had seen, that the situation was grave, and his chances of survival were not likely.

But we prayed. We prayed that God would intervene and spare my dad's life. He entered the hospital that morning, and that evening on a group call, we prayed that he would make it through the night.

He was on a BiPAP, a breathing facemask, because being intubated on a ventilator can drop the chances of survival significantly. It is basically an induced coma. At that time, the Covid ICU at Texas Health Harris Methodist Hospital of Fort Worth had seen 135 deaths with only four survivors, one from a ventilator.

The next morning, my dad's body crashed, and I got a call from my mom. "I'm on the way to the hospital. They are putting your dad on a ventilator. There's not enough time for you or your brother to get here, but you can send him a text message, and I'll make sure he reads it."

I took my phone and began texting what was likely to be the last thing I got to say to my dad. There were so many tears that my wife and I could hardly read what I was texting. I sent: "Dad, I love you more than you could possibly know."

A few moments later, we had a group FaceTime from an iPad.

We were able to see my dad, pray for him, speak words of encouragement. Then, he was placed on a ventilator.

Each day brought new complications and more bad news—lungs severely damaged, internal bleeding, no blood flow to his arms and legs. The list goes on. But we prayed.

We heard from people coming out of the woodwork who were praying for my dad—from guys he went to high school with to coworkers of mine in different states who had never met him.

One guy texted prayers to my dad's old cell number from years ago. He got this response: "This is actually not Mike's phone number anymore, but I will say, the amount of messages I've received on his behalf is pretty cool. Y'all really care for him and are praying for him, so I've been praying for him as well since the messages began."

When I look back at old text messages with my family from this time, we reference feeling a calm and peace from the Holy Spirit. That is from prayer, and we are forever grateful.

Two weeks later, my dad was able to breathe, opened his eyes again, and was off the ventilator.

The doctors couldn't explain how my dad survived these conditions; he was given the same treatment as many other patients who passed away. The doctors said it was nothing short of a miracle. We know it's from the power of prayer.

Finally, I want to talk about the power of God's plan.

My dad woke up to feet that were jet black from gangrene, a result of blood clots caused by Covid. The doctors warned that after blood is cut off from the tissue and the tissue dies, the only option is amputation. The vascular surgeon said it was unlikely he would be able to operate and blow up the remaining blood clots, but he would give it a try and see what he could do.

Our vascular surgeon is recognized in his field for operating on blood clots that others couldn't reach or wouldn't try. His nickname was "The Mad Scientist." He was exactly who we needed.

We were grateful my dad was alive, but we went back to the well for God's grace and prayed that his legs would not have to be amputated.

The surgeon operated on my dad for over two hours and said he had made more progress removing blood clots than he could have possibly imagined, and that he was able to return blood flow to the tissue in his feet.

My dad's right foot turned from black to pink, except for his toes, which were amputated. My dad's left foot did not recover, and his left leg from the knee down was scheduled to be amputated in two days.

But God's plan blessed us with another surgeon, a foot surgeon, Dr. Max Pekarev, a.k.a. Dr. Max.

Dr. Max's family immigrated from the Soviet Union to the US when he was fourteen. He attended Princeton as an undergraduate, where he was a four-time All-American, winning the NCAA Saber Fencing Championship in 1996.

He was exactly who we needed.

Even though we accepted the outcome of an amputated

leg, Dr. Max suggested an exploratory surgery before the amputation to see if there was enough tissue to save Dad's leg. He said there was a 50 percent chance of my dad waking up with an amputated leg.

After the surgery, my dad woke up to see his left leg still left intact. The doctors couldn't explain how a sixty-seven-year-old man had the muscle tissue of a teenager. This was yet another miracle.

Dr. Max suggested taking a muscle from my dad's back that would be transferred to his foot and used to reconstruct his left foot.

Our second-opinion doctor said to amputate the leg from the knee down. He explained that surgeons have tried this operation for decades with no success, not to mention the additional surgeries that would be required down the road.

Believe it or not, it seemed easier just to amputate the leg and not go down an even longer road of surgery and uncertainty, but God has a plan, and sometimes it takes faith to honor it.

The surgery was a success. He was able to keep his leg and now has a reconstructed left foot with no toes. He has been able to stand, walk, and even drive to work. He had to have similar surgeries down the road, but he got to keep his leg.

My dad spent ninety days in the hospital and has

endured eight surgeries. Some of those were small, and some were groundbreaking.

I get to call him every day. His mind is strong, and his body continues to get stronger.

There are many things I have learned from this trial. Life will hand us unimaginable circumstances, but God will give us the strength and grace we need for the day.

My dad, a.k.a. Miracle Mike, tells me, "God gives us daily bread. The grace we need *today*. Not weekly bread or monthly bread, but daily bread."

And that is the reminder I want to give you. God will give you your daily bread.

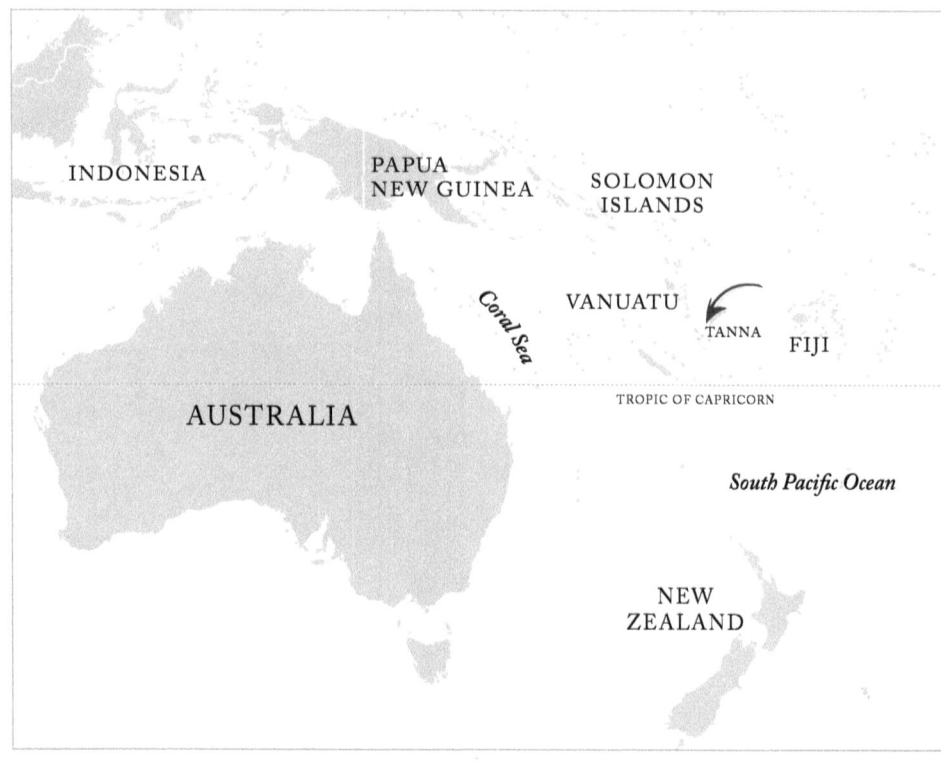

CHAPTER 20

# Do You Believe in Angels?

| | |
|---|---|
| TIME OF MIRACLE: | **Late 1800s** |
| LOCATION: | Tanna Island—New Hebrides, South Pacific |
| WITNESSES: | Reverend John Paton; his wife; the chief of a native tribe |

In his book *Angels,* Billy Graham shares how God's angels protected Reverend John G. Paton in the mission fields of New Hebrides, a group of islands in the South Pacific. Hostile natives from a cannibalistic tribe surrounded his mission headquarters one night, intending to burn the Paton's building and kill both John and his wife. John Paton and his wife were full of terror, but they prayed all night that God would protect them from harm. Daylight broke, and they were amazed to find their attackers had left. God protected them from harm. It was not until one year later when they learned how God had answered their prayers. Following the retreat from the attack, the tribe's chief had made a conversion to Christianity by accepting Christ as his personal savior.

John Paton asked the chief later what kept the tribe from attacking his mission that terror-filled night. The chief replied they had been too fearful to carry out the attack because they had seen "an army of hundreds of giant men in shiny garments with drawn swords surrounding their mission" (Graham, 1995). Only then did John

Paton realize that God had sent His angels to prevent the attack. The chief agreed that there was no other explanation.

Map of Texas showing Amarillo, El Paso, Abilene, Jacksboro, Fort Worth, Coppell, Dallas, Tyler, Austin, San Antonio, Houston, and Corpus Christi. An arrow points to Dallas.

CHAPTER 21

# *Our Protector*

| | |
|---|---|
| TIME OF MIRACLE: | **Summer of 1973** |
| LOCATION: | Dallas, Texas |
| WITNESSES: | Scott Dennis; Mike Mayo |

God provides angels to protect us when we least expect it, and when we need Him the most.

During the summer of 1973, when I was fifteen, my friend Scott Dennis and I were hired as construction laborers at an apartment complex in East Dallas. At the time, I was interested in all the extracurricular activities in school, but studying wasn't my focus. So, my father, Bill Mayo, set up our summer jobs with his developer/construction friend, Bob Hickman. He felt it would be good for me and Scott to work hard labor so we could gain an appreciation for what education could provide. We made $2.50 an hour, and our mothers had to get up early to take us to work by seven in the morning.

That summer, we met some real characters on the jobsite. Scott and I would entertain each other by imitating their odd mannerisms when they were out of sight. The language they used was quite different from the vocabulary we heard in the private Christian school we attended, but thankfully we didn't pick up any of their bad habits.

Scott and I would often find a cool, shady spot, hidden where no one could find us, to eat our sack lunches. Framing was going up at the complex, so there were many options to choose from to take a quick siesta before we were called back to our mindless jobs of pushing a broom or pulling nails.

One day as I was headed inside one of these buildings, I heard a framer yelling from the top of the roof, but I had no idea what he was trying to warn me about. While the framer had been hammering on the chimney top over three stories high, the head of his eight-pound sledgehammer had broken loose from the handle and tumbled down toward me. Eight pounds of cast iron brushed my long hair and smashed a two-inch divot into the sidewalk right next to my boot. Miraculously, the sledgehammer had missed me completely. The framer was so upset by what had happened that he packed up his tools and went home. To this day, I am totally convinced an angel deflected that sledgehammer from inflicting a serious head injury, or my early demise.

Map of Texas showing Amarillo, El Paso, Abilene, Jacksboro, Fort Worth, Coppell, Dallas, Tyler, Austin, San Antonio, Houston, and Corpus Christi. An arrow points to Coppell.

CHAPTER 22

## *Conviction*

| TIME OF MIRACLE: | **February 28, 2024** |
|---|---|
| LOCATION: | Coppell, Texas |
| WITNESSES: | Mike Mayo; Barbara Mayo; thief |

I had never felt violated in any way before until one evening on one of Coppell's coldest days in 2024 (13°F). I was working out later than usual at our neighborhood health club and had locked up all my heavy winter clothes and personal possessions in the men's locker room. After an hour of intensive weight training, it was time to relax in the hot sauna; however, when I opened my locker to retrieve my swimsuit, I found the locker was completely empty. My clothes, jacket, shoes, cell phone, house keys, car fob, and a treasured cross chain my wife had given me thirty years ago were all missing. My first thought was maybe I had just forgotten which locker I had placed my gear in. I began searching multiple lockers for my all-familiar lock, when I looked up to find a Coppell police officer standing over me investigating another theft earlier that hour. Two lockers had been hit in a short period of time within close proximity of the men's locker area. I called my wife to bring me warm clothes and an extra fob for my car. I was prompted by the officer to file a report with the police department. Even still, I had a couple of rough days worrying about the thief getting access to both my car and home.

After sharing my woes with my good friend Wayne Edson, a chaplain at the Texas Department of Criminal Justice, he said, "That person may be convicted by God when they find your cross." He was right! Two months later, two health club employees rang the doorbell of our home at eight in the morning on February 28. With huge smiles on their faces, they returned my gym bag containing all my possessions, including my cross. The person who had stolen the bag had returned my bag to the health club. Christmas had come early this year!

The night before in our men's Bible study, we had learned in John 16 about the power of the Holy Spirit and how He directly intervenes in our hearts to guide us in our daily decisions. I am happy the Holy Spirit had convicted this young man to perform a righteous act.

CHAPTER 23

# Ronald McDonald House

| TIME OF MIRACLE: | Thanksgiving 1989 |
|---|---|
| LOCATION: | East Texas |
| WITNESSES: | a boy in the fire; the boy's parents |

Following Thanksgiving week of 1989, the exploration vice president of the oil and gas company I was working with coordinated an evening for my coworkers and their spouses to volunteer at the Ronald McDonald House charity in Dallas. It was an evening I will never forget. It was a pause from our hectic work schedule as a young professional and a mother raising a toddler. Barbara, our eldest son, Josh (two at the time), and I helped serve meals to the families temporarily residing there. They could enjoy these meals at no cost to them while their family members were being treated in the nearby Parkland Hospital. That bitterly cold evening we met a family from East Texas, which I will refer to as the Jones family to protect their identity.

One week earlier, the Jones family had lost their trailer home to a devastating fire caused by a defective space heater. This family had three boys, ages two, four, and six. The parents did everything they could to protect their children from harm, but tragically all three of their boys were burned in the fire and immediately sent to Parkland Hospital, the premier burn center in the country. We were told the two-year-old baby boy had some burns to his arms and legs but survived. We learned the oldest brother perished within a couple of days of the fire. We were confident he was immediately ushered into Heaven by God. The four-year-old (Matthew) had also suffered extensive burns to his entire body but was still clinging to life. You can only imagine the grief the parents were feeling. That evening, they had very little to say and hardly made eye contact with those of us serving their meals. Their hearts had been broken. Barbara and I were also at a loss for words but tried to be encouraging by sharing with the family that they would be in our prayers.

That evening, Barbara and I returned to our warm home in Lake Highlands with heavy hearts. Before we went to bed, we peeked in several times on Josh as he was sleeping, thanking God for his health and well-being.

A couple of weeks passed, and a lady at the Ronald McDonald House called to inform us that the Joneses' middle son, Matthew, had also passed away during the night.

The funeral home in northeast Dallas (where my grandparents, father, and sister are also buried) offered the Jones family two funeral plots, caskets, and a funeral at no cost. We attended the small funeral service and heard a poem that Matthew's mother wrote. It was about a small toy soldier who kept falling and then getting back up. I vividly remember the parents gripping their youngest ever so tightly at the graveside.

Christmas of 1989 was now quickly approaching. We invited the Jones family into our home for a Christmas meal before our family showed up later that week. Barbara served her famous lasagna casserole and purchased gifts for the youngest boy and his parents. One of Barbara's love languages and strongest attributes is giving to others.

The Jones family were most gracious for the meal and the gifts, and we experienced their smiles for the first time as we watched their son and our son play with cars on our living room floor.

That special evening, we talked about the presence of God and the Holy Spirit that dwells within us when we call out to God as believers. That's when the Joneses began to open up and wanted us to know about the fire and the miracle that followed. They shared that when they visited Matthew in his hospital room at Parkland, he told his parents very calmly, and with great confidence, that he was going to be okay! The Joneses had previously been told by the burn doctor that little Matthew would most likely not survive his injuries and were perplexed by their son's comforting words, but they kept listening to what their boy had to say. Matthew told his parents that his oldest (deceased) brother and two angels had come to visit him the prior evening in his room. He was reassured by them that he was going to be okay, they would take care of him, and he would soon experience relief from his pain. Little Matthew wanted to know if he could be with them right away, but they said it would be later. He had obviously experienced and seen with his own eyes the calming, loving power of the Holy Spirit through his brother and God's special appointed angels.

All four of us were raw with emotion while they shared their story. Barbara promptly retrieved a box of tissues for the entire group. Their son had just experienced one of God's great miracles and lived long enough to tell his parents about it before he joined his brother in Heaven.

That evening, the Joneses also shared that after the graveside service for the boys, they were walking back across the cemetery grounds to their vehicle and his wife caught a glimpse of a very shiny object poking through the dirt, glistening in the sun. When she reached to pick it up, she noticed it was a Christmas ornament of a toy soldier, just like the soldier that kept getting back up in her poem she had recited. She said, "At that very moment, God had revealed to me that both of my boys were safely in Heaven and were okay!" Knowing that her boys were with God and that both parents were believers had a major impact on us. That Christmas and holiday season thirty-five years ago will never be forgotten.

Texas map showing cities: Amarillo, El Paso, Abilene, Jacksboro, Fort Worth, Coppell, Dallas, Tyler, Austin, Houston, San Antonio, Corpus Christi. An arrow points to Jacksboro.

CHAPTER 24

# *Behind the Wire*

| | |
|---|---|
| TIME OF MIRACLE: | **Summer of 2022** |
| LOCATION: | Jacksboro, Texas |
| WITNESSES: | a prison inmate; Roji Varghese |

I serve in the prison ministry with my two friends, brothers in Christ, and bodyguards, Roji and Wayne. This past summer, Roji visited a prison near Jacksboro, Texas. This particular prison has an unusual number of men who have been incarcerated due to drug addiction and for selling narcotics. The prison system has several recovery programs, one of which Wayne teaches on Wednesdays at a central Texas prison. Drugs are a vicious cycle of physical, social, and moral decay that prisoners across the state are facing. The inmates will tell you that drugs are readily available on any given day. Tragically, many die from overdose, suicide, and gang-related crime, and the prison environment has only worsened. The state is trying its very best to prevent contraband from coming in, but, unfortunately, drugs, weapons, alcohol, and cell phones still manage to find their way in.

On this particular day, Roji was preparing for an upcoming event and had the opportunity to visit with an inmate we will call Tony. Tony had a pattern of being in and out of the prison system for the last twenty-plus years. He had left behind a large path of broken relationships due to his choices to use and sell drugs. His family broke off all contact with Tony and sold or gave away all of Tony's possessions many years prior. Tony had become estranged from everyone who had once cared for him and had not had visitors in several years. Tony was a broken man that had finally hit the bottom. He had lost all hope and had become despondent. A common thread amongst many prisoners is that someone in their family, usually a mother or grandmother, recognized the destructive path they were on and told them about Christ or encouraged them to go to church. That someone would plant a seed that another later in life would try to harvest.

Tony must have had that seed already because he shared with Roji that he was ready for a life change and had sought out the prison chaplain for help. He was seeking God. He had made the first step toward a change in his life that offered hope in his lost and troubled world. The chaplain informed Tony that he should first seek out God by reading His Word.

The chaplain then informed Tony that he had permission to enter the chaplain's office and pick out a Bible of his choice for daily use. There were dozens of donated Bibles in a large tub by his desk. Tony picked the Bible on top that caught his eye and looked familiar. When he opened it up and read the inscription, he realized it was the exact same Bible his mother had given him as a boy. Tony told Roji that hot summer day that he felt like God was trying to tell him something. That something was God giving him another chance to come back to Him. God is the God of second chances.

# Closing Words

WHEN I WAS IN HIGH school at Trinity Christian Academy in Addison, Texas, our Bible professor, Lou Schneider, introduced our textbook *Evidence That Demands a Verdict*, which was originally printed in 1972. In his early life, the author, Josh McDowell, was agnostic and dead set on dispelling truths about the Bible and Jesus Christ. Josh was a well-known skeptic against Christianity; however, his historical research revealed indisputable evidence of the credibility of the Bible and Jesus Christ. Now an ambassador for Christ, Josh has written 156 books and sold over 27 million copies in 128 languages.

McDowell has spoken to more than forty-six million people in 136 countries about his faith. The Josh McDowell Ministry is a division of Campus Crusade for Christ.

In 1980, Lee Strobel was an atheist journalist and investigative reporter for the *Chicago Tribune*. Lee and Leslie Strobel's family was attending a celebratory dinner one evening when their youngest daughter choked on a piece of candy. One of the patrons in the restaurant, a nurse named Alfie, helped to save her life. Alfie gave credit to God for saving the daughter, and Lee's wife, Leslie, took it to heart. As Leslie began leaning into Christ, Lee became irritated and was determined to dissuade her about these "Christian myths." He began to gather evidence against Christ's death on the cross and His resurrection. His in-depth studies included a well-known physician with biblical and non-biblical historical data, which only proved to Lee with overwhelming evidence that Jesus had to have died on the cross. Lee continued to fight to disprove Christ; however, a well-trusted mentor explained to Lee that whether he chooses to believe or not, the last part of proving Jesus's real existence is faith. Lee decided to "take the leap of faith" and accept Christ as his personal savior. Lee later recorded his findings and wrote his best-seller book *The Case for Christ*. An inspirational movie based on his true story was produced in 2017, which is a must-see.

My mother, Delle Mayo, shared with me as a boy how I could find my own faith in Christ and where to identify the "Mayo verse" in the Bible, which has been passed down for many generations. Ephesians 2:8–9: "For it is by grace you have been saved, through faith—and this is not from yourselves, it is the gift of God—not by works, so that no one can boast."

You may wonder how God might provide a miracle in my life, or why you may not see and recognize these miracles.

Only Christ followers have the unique discernment to recognize when the Holy Spirit is working in our own personal lives as well as others. Even to those who have not committed themselves to Christ, the Holy Spirit can prick the most hardened of hearts. To become a Christ follower is an individual choice, not a privilege passed down through the family. It is not earned by good works, or by being a good person. Once one recognizes that the sin existing in their life is no longer acceptable, the acknowledgment that they can no longer bear the weight of their sins alone is the first step to salvation. It is our belief that Jesus Christ sacrificed those sins on the cross and was resurrected on the third day.

Next, those who totally let go of these sins and turn their lives completely over to Christ can begin to experience great joy with the guarantee of their salvation in Heaven after they die. In fact, those who are Christ followers never die. The Bible tells us that the moment a Christ believer takes his last breath on Earth, he simultaneously takes his first breath with Christ in Heaven. Christ created us to be with Him and worship Him forever. Here is the miraculous part: Once someone becomes a Christ follower and allows God's Holy Spirit to enter into their life, existence as it was once known will never be the same. We then have the ability to be in direct communication with God through prayer, the Bible, spiritual teaching, and words of wisdom from other fellow believers. His wisdom then begins to guide our paths through a very chaotic world.

Josh McDowell and Lee Strobel remind me of the Apostle Paul. Paul's mission in life had been to destroy Christianity by killing those who preached God's word. But once he recognized Christ and believed in Him, the scales that blinded him fell from his eyes, and when he turned to Him, only then could he see. Though he had his faults, Paul became the greatest crusader for Christ in his time, spreading the gospel through several missionary journeys in foreign lands and writing thirteen books in the New Testament.

Becoming a believer is a wonderful thing because no matter what happens in our fallen world, we have a keen perception of what occurs in the last chapter on Earth. We also know with great confidence that our names are written in the Lamb's book of life (Rev. 13:8). We have comfort in knowing we will be in there, ready to experience the rest of our lives eternally in Heaven after our short time here on Earth. We are guaranteed a spot in Heaven. As an insurance guy, the term "risk averse" is commonly used in my industry. It can apply well here with our decision to follow Christ. The Bible tells us that those who choose not to follow Christ will spend eternity in hell. I am dismayed for those whose hearts remain hardened, knowing they have ignored or simply denied Christ. Brushing off God is a very risky proposition. Biblical prophecy in the book of Revelation and from several Old Testament prophets warns us things on Earth will continue to become worse. It is guaranteed. Things of this world will perish and fade away. All of our possessions will one day be gone. Those who choose not to follow Christ will have deep regret and will be left behind in a terrible situation. Jesus tells us in the scriptures that one day Christ will return "as a thief in the night." My prayer is for you to "take that leap of faith" and be ready to meet your maker on that day.

# *Acknowledgments*

I AM SO GRATEFUL FOR THE support of my wife, Barbara, who has been encouraging and supportive throughout the writing of this book. She gave me the confidence to press forward with my vision. Forty-one years ago, I married the right woman, whose faith has been a tremendous inspiration in my personal walk. She was attending Bible studies for twenty-five years before I finally became convinced. I was just treading water spiritually and needed a deeper study to feel comfortable in sharing my faith with others. Only then did I gain an understanding of the sanctification process that, today, is still a work in progress. Barbara and I have experienced many miracles in our marriage together, including raising two great young men, Josh and Hunter. Many are not aware that she almost passed after experiencing her first childbirth. Miraculously, God saved her after several weeks of prolonged illness. It was the first of many trials that God carried us through together. God knew that I needed my soulmate to raise my boys. He also knew He was not yet done with the plans He had for her life: Christian drama, interior design, Bible study leader, ministering to others, and being a loving grandmother to her six grandchildren.

Josh and Hunter, thank you for your support during this journey. I would think of you both often when writing, reflecting on our experiences together. Several times I would pause and thank God for you. I have always been truthful, never to sugarcoat, that this old world will continue to hurl challenges your way. Stand firm, be bold and courageous. I am proud of you. Isaiah 41:10: "So do not fear, for I am with you; do not be dismayed, for I am your God. I will strengthen you; I will uphold you with my righteous right hand."

Ashleigh Allman, my lovely niece, thank you for editing my book while working as a paralegal and raising two young daughters. Your story of your mom (Leigh Ann) and Poppy (Bill Mayo) will never be forgotten in our family. I am appreciative of you sharing their stories. The legacy they left behind and the impact on our family's lives are remembered and experienced every day.

I am grateful for my good friend, Lindsey O'Connor, for allowing me to share the miraculous story of her journey after almost losing her life during childbirth. Lindsey has written five books, including *The Long Awakening*, which one of my stories is based upon. Lindsey's experience has stuck with me for many years, and I have retold her story numerous times. She has been inspirational in giving me the courage to write my own book and has been so kind to share some of her resources, like directing me to my publisher.

I am appreciative of my brother in Christ and fellow Bible study leader, Mark McKendrick, who introduced me to his father, Mike McKendrick, the Covid survivor in the story "Modern-Day Lazarus." Mike's courage and faith in God during a near-impossible survival gave me the determination to print his story so that others could share his story for many generations.

Last but not least, I am thankful for my publisher, Book Journey Publishing, and Kathleen Groom, the founder, who has patiently consulted me on the proper steps to publish my first book. Her expertise in book design, editing, customized strategic marketing, and publication has made for a smooth experience.

# *References*

Graham, Billy. 1995. *Angels: God's Secret Agents*. Nashville, TN: Thomas Nelson.

"Miracle." Wikipedia. Accessed September 19, 2025. https://en.wikipedia.org/wiki/Miracle.

O'Connor, Lindsey. 2013. *The Long Awakening: A Memoir*. Grand Rapids, MI: Revell.

Smith, William. 1995. *Smith's Bible Dictionary*. Nashville, TN: Thomas Nelson.

## *About the Author*

MIKE MAYO IS AN AUTHOR, speaker, and Bible study leader for Bible Study Fellowship and Fellowship Church prison ministries. A two-time cancer survivor, Mike has witnessed many modern-day miracles—from miraculous spiritual transformations among inmates in Texas state prisons to unexplained healings in his own community. Mike is a graduate of Baylor University and Trinity Christian Academy. He is a former commercial insurance broker and, in addition to his ministry work, enjoys traveling with his wife, Barbara, hunting, fly-fishing, golf, quality time with his sons and their families, and leisure time at his mountain cabin in Montana.

**Connect with Mike:** mikeemayo.com

www.ingramcontent.com/pod-product-compliance
Lightning Source LLC
Chambersburg PA
CBHW030243010526
44107CB00030B/1320/J